SOCIETY'S GENOME

SOCIETY'S GENOME

Genetic Diversity's Role in Digital Preservation

By Nathan Thompson
with Bob Cone and John Kranz

Cover design by Kristen Coats
Back cover image: Detail of "Ptolemy World Map," from Ptolemy's the *Geography,* redrawn by Francesco di Antonio del Chierco (15th century). Housed in the British Library, London. Image retrieved from https://commons.wikimedia.org/wiki/File:PtolemyWorldMap.jpg.

Published by Spectra Logic Corporation
6285 Lookout Road
Boulder, Colorado 80301-3580
Tel.: 1.800.833.1132
Fax: 1.303.939.8844
www.spectralogic.com

ISBN: 978-0-9975644-0-2

Printed and bound in the United States of America

10 9 8 7 6 5 4 3 2 1

This book is printed on acid-free paper.

"What is truly revolutionary about molecular biology in the post-Watson–Crick era is that it has become digital...the machine code of the genes is uncannily computer-like."

—Richard Dawkins, *River Out of Eden*

Contents

Foreword

Little is more staggering than how much information is now captured in digital form—it often feels like it encompasses practically everything. The vast archive growing globally has brought entirely new responsibilities to society. Questions such as what constitutes privacy today, what rights may exist for data to be forgotten or erased, or, in other cases, what rights may exist to capture information and retain it have a bearing on the structure of democracy itself. Global thinking about these matters is currently maturing and will lead to new practices. Moreover, defending data, or the infrastructure carrying it, from cyber threats is now as important as defending lives and land, and the scope of threats faced may be broader than what any traditional warfare has shown us.

Because these new perspectives have evolved from the technology world, it is not a surprise that companies building infrastructure for digital data have knowledge that is hard to match. They have seen firsthand how it is handled across the wide spectrum of the cloud, corporations, government, science, defense, and intelligence.

One of these companies, Spectra Logic, has been doing this for nearly 40 years, and Nathan Thompson, its founder and CEO, is the author of this book. And, yes, *Society's Genome* is a very worthwhile read. It takes the reader on a unique survey of this digital landscape, covering many interesting kinds of data, and is set against the backdrop of the responsibilities that now come with technology, the safety of data, and political governance. By the time I turned the last page, I had developed a new appreciation of how precious and rich our data really is—a genome indeed.

Peter Braam
Boulder, Colorado
April 4, 2016

A scientist, entrepreneur, and internationally recognized leader in computing and data science, Dr. Peter Braam works with research organizations, governments, and enterprises worldwide to develop innovative solutions to projects and to advance the frontiers of data technology. The founder of five successful start-ups and considered the originator of the Lustre file system, Braam is currently applying his knowledge of computing to radio astronomy, collaborating with Cambridge University on the Square Kilometre Array (SKA) Telescope Science Data Processor.

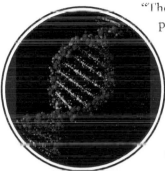

"The genome is a scripture in which is written the past history of plagues. The long struggles of our ancestors with malaria and dysentery are recorded in the patterns of human genetic variation. Your chances of avoiding death from malaria are pre-programmed in your genes, and in the genes of the malaria organism. You send out your team of genes to play the match, and so does the malaria parasite. If their attackers are better than your defenders, they win. Bad luck. No substitutes allowed."

—Matt Ridley, *Genome: The Autobiography of a Species in 23 Chapters*

Chapter 1

Survival of the Fittest...or Smartest

If history is written by the winners, then genetics documents the survivors. Since its inception, life has witnessed plagues, ice ages, meteors, and mass extinctions of every kind. Today we as a species are here, able to create and store data, only because our ancestors survived these disasters. The most powerful item in their survival toolkit was genetic diversity. Although malaria won quite a few of the matches that Matt Ridley describes in this chapter's epigraph, those individuals with an increased tolerance to the disease (or perhaps a supernatural fear of mosquitos or a penchant for cooler climates) prevailed to become the authors of future generations.

Just as human life has survived, and thrived, throughout the millennia by passing on genetic information from one generation to another, individual organizations and society at large must replicate and preserve the collective data and knowledge that defines them—their "genomes"—to function and, ultimately, to survive. If this comparison seems overwrought, consider the application of knowledge and data to modern agriculture. During the Green Revolution of the 1930s through the 1960s, the innovations pioneered by agronomist Norman Borlaug and his fellow scientists increased global agricultural yields by an incredible amount. Without the development of high-yield, disease-resistant dwarf wheat, it is believed that a billion people would have starved (or would not have been born at all).[1] In another example, recent developments in prescriptive planting have set the stage for using Big Data techniques to increase agricultural yields by an additional 25 percent without the alteration of seed, water, or fertilizer use:

> Big agricultural companies say the next revolution on the farm will come from feeding data gathered by tractors and other machinery into computers that tell farmers how to increase their output of crops like corn and soybeans. Monsanto Co., DuPont Co., and other companies are racing to roll out "prescriptive planting" technology to farmers across the U.S. who know from years of experience that tiny adjustments in planting depth or the distance between crop rows can make a big difference in revenue at harvest time.[2]

Advancements such as these in agriculture illustrate how our survival as a society requires the preservation of our society's genome, the vast collective body of data created by both individuals and organizations. Just as an organism's genome is a "recipe" to propagate copies of itself, society's genome is a recipe to propagate modernity. Should a large portion of this recipe be suddenly lost, society could regress. Although a cataclysmic descent into a new dark age is unlikely, lost or forgotten information has led to substantive setbacks in technological progress and it may do so again.

Society is inextricably dependent on technology for its basic needs, and so it is vital that its genome is preserved and protected from evolutionary, epochal threats. For modern data centers—the keepers of this genome, and by extension, modernity itself—the threats are far-reaching and complex. For humanity, they pose a challenge without precedent. Our species has access to and depends on more information now than in its entire existence. Ensuring that this data can be retrieved by future generations is one of the greatest priorities of our time. The natural history of life itself serves as the best teacher here, and its lesson is clear: Genetic diversity is the key to survival. Ensuring genetic diversity in data storage is just as necessary for the long-term survival of the information upon which our civilization is built.

Recorded history offers little instruction on how to best manage data on the scale it is being created today, but it does provide sober reminders of what can happen when we fail to preserve information for the future. In 150 CE in Alexandria, Egypt, Roman scholar Claudius Ptolemy completed the *Geography*, a magnificent compilation of the geographic knowledge of the second-century Roman Empire. His work was based on a lost atlas by Marinus of Tyre that contained coordinates of the world as the Romans knew it—from the Fortunate Isles in the Atlantic Ocean to the middle of China (then called Serica, the land of silk). To this atlas, Ptolemy added mathematical projection methods. All told, about 80 degrees of latitude and 180 degrees of longitude were included, yielding a flawed but navigable map (Figure 1). Even with errors of mathematical projection and mistaken geographic beliefs, the knowledge contained within Ptolemy's map was likely important to the Roman Empire's expansion. According to Wikipedia: "Trade throughout the Indian Ocean was extensive from the second century, and many Roman trading ports have been identified in India. From these ports, Roman embassies to China are recorded in Chinese historical sources from around 166."[3]

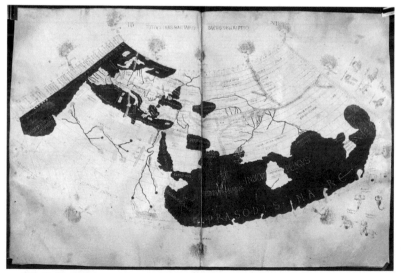

Fig. 1 Ptolemy's world map, redrawn by Francesco d'Antonio del Chierico (15th century).

Unfortunately, this knowledge was completely lost with the fall of the Roman Empire. While the Byzantine monk Maximus Planudes is believed to have reassembled a Ptolemaic map in Constantinople in 1295 CE (a re-creation of it is shown on this book's back cover), the map and the *Geography* were not recovered and translated into Latin until 1407. Navigation and trade were hampered for more than a thousand years as a result.

Other examples of lost ancient knowledge include the Bakhshali Manuscript, an Indian work of mathematics written in Sanskrit on birch bark, that was "a collection of computational, arithmetical, and algebraic algorithms and simple problems" dating perhaps as far back as Ptolemy's map. Although a copy was found in 1881, it is incomplete and too fragile to be examined by scholars.[4] In 1424, the willful destruction by Hongxi Emperor of the treasure ships led by his admiral, Zheng He, curtailed voyages that were "a floating encyclopedia-in-progress for Ming China—a compilation of all worth knowing between Nanjing and Africa."[5]

For hundreds or perhaps a thousand years, much of this information, as with much knowledge of the ancient era, was lost to scholars, traders, and navigators. How much more dangerous would it be then to lose substantive geographic data in the age of GPS? Maintaining multiple copies protects data against most traditional threats and has been an important part of data survival since long before punch cards. It is a perfect defense against missteps involving data management, such as human error or improper handling. When a file is accidentally deleted or a lid flies off a Starbucks cup, having a backup copy somewhere is all that stands between inconvenience and permanent loss. This is the traditional role of backup storage.

The modern data center, however, not only has orders of magnitude more data to deal with than older data centers ever did, it must also protect data against malfeasance, including the willful destruction of data, equipment, and infrastructure. The stakes are higher and the threats are more diverse. The good news, however, is that we can find the tools and strategies to solve these problems. This book does this by taking the unique approach of looking to the natural world for insights into how diversity can ensure long-term survival, and to apply that key principle to the countering of modern data threats, for which redundancy is no longer enough.

In the natural world, diversity plays a key role in an evolutionary system. Consider birds living in an isolated habitat, such as on a remote island. If an extended drought wipes out the normal food supply, those birds with the sharpest beaks and hardest skulls would be most likely to survive because they would be able to access food supplies that other birds could not, such as insects living underneath tree bark. Should the habitat flood, birds with longer legs could be expected to survive by wading into the water and eating aquatic insects or small fish. In either case, a species with diverse traits is better positioned to respond to unexpected events, allowing some members of its species to continue and to pass on their genomes to future generations.

While animals generally cannot consciously "select for" their basic physical features, there are many examples of diversity, or lack thereof, where choice *is* involved. Recognizing the value of diversity, as applied to the evolutionary system of information technology (IT) and the modern data center, is the best way that we can make the right choices for protecting information and ensuring that it is passed on to future generations.

Bloodline and Famine: Lessons for a Digital Age

In the mid-19th century, Great Britain was a superpower, however its reigning monarch was facing a grave personal challenge. For generations, Queen Victoria's royal ancestors had practiced cousin marriage, which continued into her own reign through her marriage to first cousin Prince Albert. Genetic homogeneity produced hemophilia in her, as it did in other members of the royal family. Compared to their genetically diverse subjects, they lived their lives at heightened risk, for even a small wound could bleed profusely and lead to death.

During the queen's reign, another kind of inbreeding plagued Ireland, appearing not in royal form, but in the humble soil of Irish farmlands. In the early 19th century, Ireland's population was increasing rapidly, leading the populace to farm the lumper potato, *Solanum tuberosum,* as a primary—and in many cases, only—food source. By 1840, the Irish were relying on this single species for their sustenance, growing it by planting a piece of another potato plant, "essentially growing clones of only a few varieties. As a result, when the blight reached Ireland on ships traveling between America and Britain, *Phytophthora infestans* rapidly spread through Ireland, resulting in the devastating famine."[6]

Virtually every potato that might have matured in Ireland's fields instead turned to slime. The subsequent, nearly decade-long

Great Famine killed at least one million people, with another two million leaving the country in desperation. The repercussions of the famine were felt for decades on both humanitarian and political levels. The muted British response brought down the government of Prime Minister Robert Peel, accelerated emigration to America, and laid the foundation for Irish Republicanism and Ireland's eventual independence.

The impaired health of the royal family and the devastation of the Great Famine demonstrate one indisputable fact: If we ignore the imperative for genetic diversity, we place ourselves at greater risk. With diversity comes strength and resilience. Today, however, we are turning a blind eye to a lack of genetic diversity in a new realm—a cyber world of our own creation. The data storage used by our institutions and upon which our daily lives rely is falling prey to genetic homogeneity. As with Queen Victoria and her ancestors, our storage methods are too closely related—they lack sufficient diversity. And as seen in the agricultural short-sightedness that precipitated a humanitarian tragedy, society's genome—the information that feeds and sustains us as a civilization—can be vulnerable to eradication by a single attack.

Too Much of a Good Thing?

Until recently, homogeneity was not an issue for the Information Age. The IT era is a young one, having thrived in its earliest days on a volatile influx of competitive, disparate technologies and IT methodologies that were constantly changing at a rate that ensured a diverse offering of products. Growth and maturity, however, have led the industry to consolidate its manufacturers and procedures over time, much of it done by commoditizing most of the storage sector. This has reduced costs, simplified procedures, and allowed for exponential growth. However, consolidation is rarely rewarded in evolution, and so the industry now faces a set of challenges, dangers, and potential disasters that were highly unlikely in its early days.

In 1995, a data center could store and process volumes of information that tallied in gigabytes. Information was stored across a range of media (such as various types of tapes, hard drives, and other backup systems). Were one medium to fail, another could supplant it. Data backups were also kept in a variety of super-secure locations around the world—not just in a 100-mile-radius cloud, as is common today. Fire, floods, earthquakes, war, or other disasters might destroy a few select locations, but no disaster could touch all of them. These data centers were also disciplined in creating multiple copies of data, storing those copies on different media types and sending at least one copy offsite for disaster recovery. The approach was the forerunner to what is often referred to as the "3-2-1" rule: Make at least three copies of your data, store the data on at least two different types of media, and maintain at least one copy offsite.

In this manner, the data centers of 20 years ago ingeniously maintained genetic diversity, like a young evolutionary ecosystem. First, they used a mix of different media and locations to maximize information security. Next, they recognized, understood, and planned for worst-case scenarios. Finally, they were always prepared to rebuild from the ground up if they had to, using the information they had protected from disaster to do so. In the 1990s, backup and archiving processes were still in their infancy, yet the basic principles practiced then remain valid today.

However, in some fundamental ways, the protocols of a 1995 data center have been weakened or negated. Today capacities have expanded to include weekly data volumes in the hundreds of terabytes, petabytes, and beyond. Specialization and consolidation have played major roles in increased cost savings and the economic availability of storage today. In fact, the storage cost curve rivals that of the speed, power, and size improvements seen in microprocessors. It is important to note, however, that this consolidation has introduced new risks.

While it is easy to think of storage in terms of media (disk versus tape, for example) or brand (IBM, Dell, Spectra Logic, HP, and so on), consolidation has meant that an apparent diversity in storage brands does not reflect the more homogeneous nature of storage technologies behind the brands. For instance, in the 1990s, there were more than 70 manufacturers of tape drives; today there are three. Disk drive consolidation is about the same—from dozens of types in the 1980s and 1990s to just three today, with only two of the three still being players in the enterprise storage market (Figure 2).

In a way, consolidation and standardization have made enterprise disk drives a modern-day lumper potato. As Chapter 5 will discuss, malware designed to attack disk firmware would only need to succeed against the products of two manufacturers to wipe out roughly 90 percent of all enterprise disk drives in existence. Similarly, tape choices have coalesced to three formats: LTO (created by the LTO Consortium), TS (introduced by IBM), and T10000x (created by Oracle), which has created comparable vulnerabilities for tape technology. Although we cannot control consolidation in manufacturing, and for the most part do not want to, the consolidation of all disks, tapes, and optical drives used for archive storage can be offset by using a combination of these technologies. In this manner, we can leverage the strengths of each to prevent further risks.

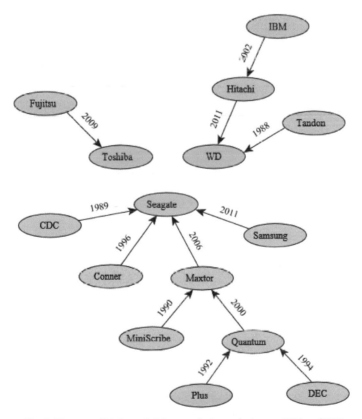

Fig. 2 The consolidation of disk manufacturers between 1989 and 2011. (WD refers to Western Digital.)

The Gamble...and the Stakes

Today the availability and ease of IT and online services have profoundly changed the world socially, politically, and economically, opening exciting new frontiers that few companies and individuals would willingly reject. At the same time, however, this technological progress has opened a Pandora's box of potential pitfalls, problems, and catastrophes. Are we ready to deal with all of them? Unfortunately, signs point to no.

A recent study by the research firm International Data Corporation (IDC) reveals that 42 percent of data in the United States that should require security has none.[7] Worldwide, the number jumps to 47 percent. The question is not if—but when—a data catastrophe will occur. What is then at stake? Society depends on the knowledge in its genome for a huge range of vital services, many of which are taken for granted:

- Communications
- Energy generation
- The power grid
- Air and other transportation
- National defense
- Commerce and finance
- Distribution and inventory systems
- Health and medical systems

These entities require access to data in order to function. Leaving aside the mass disruptions that would occur throughout the public and private sectors, the financial costs alone of data loss are staggering. A recent study by the Aberdeen Group, a U.S. technology and research services company, places the average cost of downtime due to data loss at more than $163,000 per hour; larger companies report hourly costs of more than $680,000.[8] And these are companies that eventually regained their data access. How could we even begin to calculate the value of information irretrievably lost?

In *Society's Genome*, we find that many of the laws of nature used to ensure survival also apply to data protection. A single species of plant stands a better chance of survival when there are multiple varieties of that species. Similarly, we see that a variety of digital storage media creates robustness in the data center, as the weakness of one storage type is offset by the strengths of another.

Nature also shows us the importance of having multiple copies of information—plants produce thousands of identical seeds—and the need for diversity in the geographic dispersal of information—seeds are moved by wind, insects, or animals to a myriad of landing spots. The likelihood that any one seed will mature into an adult plant is small to infinitesimal, yet plants thrive.

Likewise, multiple copies of digital content stored in diverse locations will stand a better chance of survival. And just as accurate replication of DNA is essential to the lives of cells and other biological organisms, nature has become expert at accurate replication. A healthy cell can transform into a cancerous cell if its DNA is not accurately copied. In data storage, we use hash codes, error correction, and bit recovery to ensure accurate reproduction.

Our stewardship of data and information determines our future. If society's genome were destroyed, fully rebuilding it would prove impossible. A secure, incorruptible archive of information and knowledge is a must. Fortunately, nature's toolkit has answers for addressing the hazards facing both organizations and users, and these will be discussed in later chapters.

First, however, we must more closely examine the stakeholders at risk, and they are not just the companies of the world. More and more of the information that organizations are handling is being created by individuals. In 2012, an amazing 68 percent of the content found in the digital universe was created and used by individual consumers, yet the majority of that information wound up in corporate data centers.[9] And as we will see in the next chapter, this data has become integral to daily life, making organizations—whether they are willing to be or not—increasingly responsible for the protection and stewardship of society's genome at large.

"Today there is an implicit belief among technologists that big data traces its lineage to the silicon revolution. That simply is not so. Modern IT systems certainly make big data possible, but at its core the move to big data is a continuation of humankind's ancient quest to measure, record, and analyze the world."

—Viktor Mayer-Schönberger and Kenneth Cukier, *Big Data: A Revolution That Will Transform How We Live, Work and Think*

Chapter 2

The Evolution of Revolution

A buzz phrase these days, the Internet of Things (IoT) describes the rapid and ongoing integration of the physical world with computer-based systems through electronics, sensors, and network connectivity. For society as a whole, the IoT is revolutionizing manufacturing, transportation, healthcare systems, military operations, entertainment, and other major sectors of business and government.

For us as individuals, the IoT has allowed digital access to enter into, and even reshape, virtually every aspect of our lives. We have Internet access to our friends, family, cars, home appliances, fitness wristbands, TVs, medical devices, home heating and air, lights, locks, garage doors, and so on, and the breadth and depth of permeation is astounding. Consider the events of just one hour in the life of a typical American adult connected to the IoT. Let us call him "Steve."

A Day in the Digital Life of Steve

- **4:50 a.m.** The heating system turns up the house temperature from 65°F to 70°F.
- **5:00 a.m.** The coffeemaker turns on.
- **5:15 a.m.** The alarm clock goes off, waking Steve.
- **5:20 a.m.** The radio begins playing "Chopin's Spring Waltz."
- **5:30 a.m.** A Web application alarm prompts the toaster to toast two slices of bread.
- **5:32 a.m.** After his shower, Steve steps onto the bathroom scale, which tells him his weight and body fat composition.
- **5:33 a.m.** A pill bottle in the medicine cabinet chimes. Steve opens the door to see the lid of his blood-pressure medicine bottle glowing. He forgot to take his pill last night.
- **5:34 a.m.** Steve speaks into his smartwatch, "Note to self: Download Mom's blood-pressure meds history. She has been complaining about dizzy spells. Second note to self: Run a self-test on Mom's slippers. They have not notified me if she has had trouble walking." Steve's smartwatch duly records both notes.

- **5:37 a.m.** A loud buzzing is coming from the closet. It is Steve's fitness wristband. He puts it on, not wanting to lose the calorie count he will get from going downstairs.
- **5:38 a.m.** The toaster texts Steve: "The toast is done."
- **5:40 a.m.** Steve's watch alerts him that his drive time on Route 1 will be tight. He grabs his toast, pours his coffee into his thermal-regulating mug, and heads out to work.
- **5:41 a.m.** Sensing that the door has been unlocked and relocked, the heating system returns the house temperature to 65°F.

In under an hour, well before six a.m., Steve's digital world has already exploded into millions of binary ones and zeroes, the language of digital information. Some context can help here. As those who deal with digital technology know, each one or zero is a bit, and eight bits make a byte. A kilobyte (KB) is made up of 1,024 bytes, 1,024 KB is a megabyte (MB), 1,024 MB equals a gigabyte (GB), and 1,024 GB equals a terabyte (TB). The progression continues with less common prefixes: petabytes (PB), exabytes (EB), and zettabytes (ZB). After that come yottabytes and other progressively larger data sizes (xenottabytes, shilentnobytes, and on and on). As Chapter 4 will detail, counting society's genome in zettabytes will suffice for many years to come.

So what else will happen in Steve's day? He will be notified every time his garage door opens and closes by strategically placed cameras that record, and text to him, the movements of anyone entering or leaving his home. And thanks to GPS tracking via cell phone, he will be notified whenever his daughter's boyfriend comes within 30 feet of her. He will scan Facebook to learn what his children are thinking and doing, and may even see pictures of their activities. While checking on his kids, he will see several ads customized specifically to match his age, gender, and interests, all based on his Internet browsing history.

As an individual creator of data, Steve will also contribute to the worldwide generation of digital information in his own personal way. Each day on average, he will send 28 texts, receive 33 texts, log in to five separate digital accounts, take 14 photos, and link to more than 110 individual Internet-connected devices. Many of his transactions will generate only small amounts of data and have relatively modest storage requirements, but others will require much larger amounts of data. For example, creating and sharing 4K video requires terabytes. *The Economist*

notes, "In raw form, a two-and-a-half-hour film shot in 4K at the usual 24 frames per second contains 216,000 frames. With each frame of the film containing 8.6 million pixels, and each pixel having 24 bits of color information, the resulting video file contains 5.6 terabytes of data."[1]

How Big Is Big?

IDC estimates that by the year 2020, the digital world will have created 40 zettabytes of information. That is a little over five terabytes for every man, woman, and child who will be alive in 2020.[2] If this information were put into books, 40 zettabytes' worth would make up more than 2,900 stacks, each reaching 93 million miles—the distance to the sun.[3]

According to IDC, roughly 80 percent of this astounding amount of generated data will actually be stored. When predicting data growth and retention, it is easy to kick the can down the road by assuming that storage is a problem for the future. But the future is here. How much of the technology in Steve's morning is futuristic and how much of it is available today? The answer may surprise you: All of it exists now. Yes, even the slippers. Developed by AT&T, which is working with Texas Instruments and a company called 24eight, Smart Slippers technology measures foot pressure, stride, and general mobility to yield data that can be used in many healthcare applications, including predicting and preventing falls, identifying changes in activity, and tracking progress in physical therapy.[4]

Welcome to the Digital Revolution. It is more than just a catchphrase to throw out at dinner parties when talking about your third-grader's Scratch programming class. And it does not only apply to Fortune 500 companies. Organizations of every size and type are affected, as are individuals from virtually every walk of life. We are in this together. Data creation impacts every aspect of our personal and professional lives, defining our perceptions and expectations and transforming how we communicate with each other. Immersed as we are in this technology, however, it can be hard to grasp the true scope of the changes afoot. To understand their full implications, we must look back at the world as it was before the Digital Revolution began.

From Steam Engines to Search Engines

The Industrial Revolution, which unfolded between the mid-18th and mid-19th centuries, marked an important period of transition to new manufacturing processes. The events of this period have filled countless textbooks, but it is important to emphasize that it was about more than just the invention of new machines and production techniques. Just as important was the way in which industrialization transformed the fabric of broader society through its profound impact on working conditions, urbanization, living standards, and the social roles of women and children. Advances in technology brought incredible wealth to industrializing societies. For the first time in world history a true middle class emerged from poverty, forever altering the economic and social structures of our world.

The electrification of factories, the introduction of the assembly line, and the advent of mass production marked the second phase of the Industrial Revolution, also known as the

Technological Revolution (c. 1860–1900), which launched society into a new economy, one driven by some 70 subsequent years of ongoing and rapid technological changes. After this revolution began, however, several decades passed before there was once again a measurable increase in overall productivity. From the point of view of standard growth models, this delay is puzzling. However, historians hypothesize that it was due to the slow diffusion of new technologies among manufacturing plants and to the sluggish pace of ongoing training in these plants after new technologies were adopted. The reluctance of manufacturers to abandon their accumulated expertise in old technologies—embodied in the design of existing plants—slowed the diffusion of new technologies for decades.[5]

In contrast, the metaphoric Digital Revolution differs from its industrial counterpart in one especially fundamental way—sheer speed. This modern-day revolution is not being driven by manufacturers and their factories, which have traditionally set the pace, but by individuals themselves, many of whom are under the age of 21—the early adopters and quickly shifting trendsetters who were born into the Digital Revolution. This is not to say that older generations are far behind them. In fact, technology is being embraced at a rapid pace across nearly all demographic profiles.

What is also notable is the stunning contrast between the rate of adoption of older communication technologies and that of newer digital technologies. For example, it took the telephone 25 years to go from availability to 10-percent market penetration. It took almost another 40 years to progress to 40-percent market penetration. In contrast, it took the smartphone roughly eight years to reach penetration of 10 percent and another approximately two-and-a-half years to reach 40 percent. The Internet hit 10-percent penetration in nine years and attained 40 percent in another five.[6]

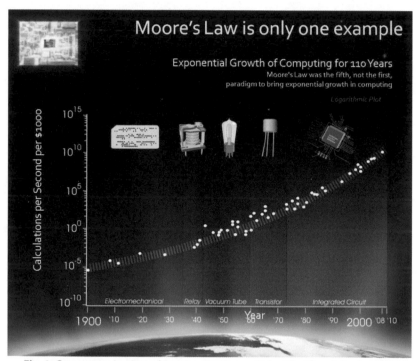

Fig. 1 Computer scientist and inventor Ray Kurzweil identified five distinct paradigms for correlating exponential computing growth to the price-performance of computing, going back to 1900.

Supporting these rapid rates of adoption, as well as increased demands for access, is the continued exponential growth of computing power. Cofounder of Intel Corporation, Gordon E. Moore coined his eponymous "Moore's Law" in 1965, with a paper projecting that the number of transistors on integrated circuits would double every year for a decade. When that decade passed, he slowed the doubling to every two years. Although the exact rates and dates have been topics of discussion, exponential growth in the semiconductor industry has been surprisingly durable. We expect this trend to continue and have seen similar growth rates in other areas of technology. Figure 1 illustrates the correlation between exponential growth of computing and price performance.

Social, Cultural, and Political Change

The speed at which new technologies are being adopted is just one important aspect of the Digital Revolution. The speed of communication, including its impact on global society, is another. The evolution of communication capabilities has left no group untouched—from individuals to corporations to governments, new communication speeds have changed everything.

The Digital Revolution has even played a powerful role in facilitating actual revolution. Putting millions of cell phones embedded with cameras and connected to the Internet into the hands of individuals throughout the Middle East was pivotal to the unfolding of the Arab Spring. University of Washington performed in-depth research on the role of social media in the uprisings held across Egypt, Tunisia, Libya, Syria, Morocco, Yemen, Algeria, and elsewhere. Information collected from Facebook, Twitter, and YouTube, with shed light on a new order of communication made possible by such digital outlets. Figure 2 also shows another study by Northwestern University.

According to the University of Washington study, the key demographic group using social media during the uprisings was composed of "young, urban, relatively well-educated individuals, many of whom were women."[7] This is not the typical voice we expect to hear coming out of the Middle East. Bloggers were able to publish negative critiques of governments on the Web, and political organizations took this information and disseminated it to broader audiences via Western outlets such as CNN and the BBC.

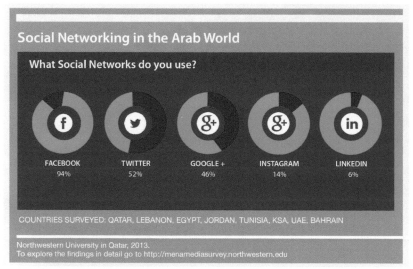

Fig. 2 A survey of eight Arab countries conducted by Northwestern University showing most-used social media outlets.

According to the report, "over the course of a week before [Egyptian President] Mubarak's resignation, the total rate of tweets from Egypt—and around the world—about political change in that country ballooned from 2,300 tweets a day to 230,000 a day."[8] It is hard not to see the correlation between the unprecedented digital communication that preceded the revolution and the unprecedented political change that soon followed it.

The political impact of this technology has not been lost on Western leaders. U.S. President Barack Obama opened a

Twitter account in March 2007 and has used Twitter for everything from promoting legislation to holding Twitter-based town hall meetings. In December 2014 he was one of only three Twitter account holders with more than 50 million followers, sharing the honor with Katy Perry and Justin Bieber.

President Obama also grew his Twitter following faster than any individual or group before him, with one million followers in the first four and a half hours after creating his account. He held that position until mid-2015, when Caitlyn Jenner, a transgender woman (the Olympic gold medalist formerly known as Bruce Jenner), picked up one million followers in only four hours. Barely a year prior, transgenderism was rarely discussed in mainstream media. Thusly the revolution proceeds from having a political impact to a social impact to a cultural impact. That a transgender individual can attract the attention of one million people in four hours says a lot about how the Digital Revolution has changed our daily lives and culture.

One institution that does recognize the impact of this revolution in communication is the Library of Congress (LOC). It considered the impact of digital communication outlets to be significant enough to request that all previous tweets recorded by Twitter, as well as any ongoing tweets, be housed in LOC archives as a historical record of American culture. According to Gayle Osterberg, the LOC's director of communications, the LOC has "an archive of approximately 170 billion tweets and growing. The volume of tweets that the library receives each day has grown from 140 million beginning in February 2011 to nearly half a billion tweets each day as of October 2012."[9] Tweets are not the only digital information that the LOC stores:

> *The Library has been collecting materials from the Web since it began harvesting congressional and presidential campaign websites in 2000 . . . including legal blogs, websites of candidates for national office, and websites of members of Congress.*[10]

As of 2012 the LOC estimated that it held three petabytes of digital information.[11] To put this in perspective, "One petabyte of data is equivalent to all of the (nondigital) content in the U.S. Library of Congress—by its own claim the largest library in the world—multiplied by 50."[12] Archiving massive amounts of digital information is an important concern for the LOC, as Osterberg points out. "The library's focus now is on addressing the significant technology challenges to making the archive accessible to researchers in a comprehensive, useful way."[13]

Society Takes a Selfie

Although the Library of Congress may be ahead of the curve in making its vast digital archive accessible, more and more organizations, from private firms to nongovernmental organizations, are grappling with their own challenges of data storage and accessibility in the face of the unprecedented amount of digital information they are collecting.

While the data related to political revolutions and social change is making headlines, the more "mundane," daily activities of everyday people are also being digitally recorded. Shopping behaviors are captured every second through transaction receipts, traffic flow is measured through toll cameras, and Web-search captures record the product preferences of millions of people. The list is endless, and this all-encompassing information gathering highlights another key difference between the Digital Revolution and the Industrial Revolution.

Specifically, the Industrial Revolution was defined by its output: automobiles, factories, consumer products, and other industrial items. And although it undisputedly changed culture in dramatic ways, it recorded very little about the culture that it was changing. The act of building a car does not provide information about the consumer who will eventually buy the car.

In contrast, the Digital Revolution, is not only self-perpetuating, it is self-recording. In other words, the technology driving it is the same technology being used to document it. Digital recording is the single greatest output of the Digital Revolution, by size and, quite likely, by importance.

It is this exponential proliferation of data, in every conceivable category, that has led to a whole new industry of computer software, hardware, and expertise known as "data analytics," which involves examining data to uncover correlations and patterns than can yield insights. Countless articles and numerous books have been written on what is referred to as "Big Data." The McKinsey Global Institute believes that, "the use of Big Data will become a key basis of competition, underpinning new waves of productivity growth, innovation, and consumer surplus."[14]

Doubtless we are living in heady technological times. However, in the face of the relentless and the ever-increasing creation, pursuit, and capture of data and the exponential growth of computing power, it is often forgotten that there is no value in data collection if the data is not protected and accessible. The need to store digital information has gone from holding a few years' worth of material, usually dictated by federal compliance or regulation, to holding data virtually forever for its powerful, predictive ability. This book will not add to the burgeoning literature on Big Data and data analytics, aside from briefly touching on these topics in Chapter 4. Rather, it is intended to explore how we will hold and retrieve the zettabytes of data being created—uncorrupted and unabridged—in the coming decades.

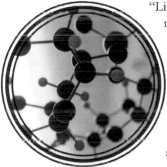

"Living organisms, [Steve Grand] declares, are made not of atoms and molecules but rather of cycles of cause and effect. They happen to use atoms and molecules, but this is not essential. Stuart Kauffman enunciated a similar view in regard to networks of gene expression. Life, at its root, he said, 'lies in the property of catalytic closure among a collection of molecular species. Alone, each molecular species is dead. Jointly, once catalytic closure among them is achieved, the collective system of molecules is alive.'"

—Dennis Bray, *Wetware: A Computer in Every Living Cell*

Chapter 3

The Genome of a Corporation

Just as individuals have "digital lives," so do organizations. It would be virtually impossible to list all of the "nonindividuals" that create, collect, use, redirect, and even monetize digital information, but they do include both private- and public-sector corporations, education and research facilities, retailers, manufacturers, media and entertainment companies, universities, and healthcare providers—essentially any group that creates, stores, and requires data to complete its mission.

The digital life of an individual is a marker for where the individual has been. The paper trail of the 1990s has been replaced by the digital trail of the 21st century. While not a perfect analogue for DNA—data does not create the next organism in a genea-logical procession—digital information has become important in the incremental, evolutionary progression of individuals.

But what about organizations? Is this where two digital lives—that of an individual and that of a corporation—part ways? We often say that people "are what they eat." For organiza-tions the adage is slightly different: You are what you compute. The digital life of the organization is, in effect, its genome because the information that an organization creates or cap-tures now represents the organization. Without the ability to access the data, however, most organizations would have the same chance at survival as an organism that could not access its genetic code.

The genome of an organization is passed along in many different ways. Long-standing organizations might pass on their genome from one generation of leaders to the next. Some companies might merge with other companies, at which point their genome changes in line with the new information they now have access to. But then there are the organizations that never manage to pass on their genomes, and there are many causes for this, including a lack of financial viability, the presence of fierce competition, or the lack of need for their service or product. Another reason can be the complete and permanent loss of organizational information as a result of a natural or man-made disaster. Whatever the reason, like organisms trapped in isolation or unable to adapt to their environments, many groups simply cease to exist, with the information they hold dying along with them.

The Humanity of Preserving Knowledge

In his book, *The Rational Optimist,* Matt Ridley points out that humans are the only species of animal that passes knowledge and information from one generation to the next for it to be built upon and improved.[1] This is how cultures, governments, and organizations of all types evolve. Because humankind is so dependent on the cultural traditions, social norms, governments, and private organizations created through this process, it can be said with little exaggeration that the survival of global society as we know it depends on preserving and passing along society's genome, the information of our past and present and the blueprint critical to ensuring the best possible future.

Knowledge and information may play vital roles in our global civilization, but not all information is created equal or holds the same value. Contrast, for example, the digital information used to report the current temperature in your home with the digital information used to collect and record the air temperature and weather trends of your hometown over an entire decade. The first piece of information will benefit you on a hot summer day or a cold winter night. The second will be fed into models that can predict long-range weather patterns for years to come. The utility of predicting weather patterns for agriculture, coastal dwellers, and urban planners outweighs—at least for society at large—the value of knowing that your house's temperature is set at a comfortable 72 degrees.

This is actually quite similar to the human genome. Not every piece of information that gets passed along is demonstrably necessary. Our fifth toe (or "pinky toe") has arguably very little value, and the appendix has been described as "just a useless remnant from our evolutionary past. Surgical removal of the appendix causes no observable health problems."[2] As we discuss the importance of digital information and the role it plays in today's world, it is important to distinguish between the different types of information we create and, when possible, assess the value of each type. In his book, *The Evolution of Everything: How New Ideas Emerge*, Ridley contrasts the "junk" with the "garbage" found in human DNA:

> As Sydney Brenner later made plain, people everywhere make the distinction between two kinds of rubbish: "garbage" which has no use and must be disposed of lest it rot and stink, and "junk," which has no immediate use but does no harm and is kept in the attic in case it might one day be put back to use. You put garbage in the rubbish bin; you keep junk in the attic or garage.[3]

The human genome keeps and copies much material that is, at least to us, not obviously beneficial to the host organism. Data storage personnel may see the parallels between the material they handle and human DNA. Junk is stored with the expectation of future use. Unexpected relationships appear in Big Data analysis only because seemingly disparate data was kept around long enough to process. This was how retailers discovered the surprising correlation of the sales of Pop Tarts and hurricane preparations, or that pregnancies can be predicted by the purchase of unscented lotion (see Chapter 4).[4] The Big Data techniques being used to uncover these statistical relationships assume that one cannot know beforehand which data sets will be of interest.

Genome Preservation Versus Backup

The creation, storage, and protection of data has been ongoing for many decades, however the idea that data should be kept indefinitely for purposes of deriving new value from it at some point in the future is a relatively new concept. Traditional data protection operated under a different paradigm, and to understand this transition it is best to briefly review what is referred to as general information technology, or general IT.

General IT is often used to describe daily digital business operations, which typically include managing an organization's e-mail, communication networks, departmental and employee-used applications, websites, and so forth. Backing up data or making copies to protect an organization's assets from viruses or accidental deletion and providing for disaster recovery has been at the core of data management in general IT for decades.

Although they have never been considered exciting, backups have always been important. The typical corporation requires weekly full backups of all digital data, as well as daily backups of any data that has been changed since the last full backup. Procedures for disaster recovery may resemble those for backups, but they serve a different purpose, such as in the case of a catastrophic data loss due to a fire, flood, earthquake, or other destructive force, whereupon the disaster recovery copy is used to restore data. However, recovery only works if the copy is stored in a location away from the disaster. If a wide geographic area has been affected, then the recovery copy would need to have been stored farther away than the building next door, or even the other side of town.

This is not new information to anyone familiar with IT, since it is a traditional approach to satisfying a universal need in data protection. It is important to directly reference this practice, however, because in many cases it has become the model for accommodating new needs in data protection, despite it not always being the best answer to addressing those needs.

Throughout the first decade of this century, the use of backups was focused on recreating the past. If a file was corrupted or accidentally deleted, its owner would want the information restored in its original form and in its most recent iteration. Multiple copies of each file are generated by repeating backups on a daily and weekly basis, but the value of a backup copy greatly diminishes each time a more recent copy is created. Why restore a file that is months old when last night's copy is available? Regardless, IT departments wisely keep many copies just in case a bug creeps in and is not discovered until weeks or months later.

Unfortunately, it is costly to manage data that includes files that are rarely if ever used, and whose value diminishes over time. But many organizations are not allowed to decide for themselves how long they must keep copies of information, since numerous federal and industry regulations mandate how long data must be kept. In the healthcare industry, HIPAA compliance requires that patient records be stored from 21 years of age to life. SEC Rule 17a-4 requires brokerages or securities exchange houses to retain certain information for six or more years. OSHA, Sarbanes-Oxley, and international regulations, such as the European General Data Protection

Regulation, have something to say about how long data should be retained.

The data falling under these watchful eyes is typically referred to as "compliance data," and it is often targeted in lawsuits of all types. The dreaded process of "e-discovery" refers to the dredging through of inordinate amounts of archived digital information that could go back for many years. It is all stored for the sake of later discovery as relevant information to be turned over to opposing counsel during litigation or governmental investigations.[5] If that does not sound good, it is because for many IT professionals it is not. Having to restore a large data set just to fulfill legal requirements takes up resources that could be better used in advancing IT capabilities. These are the historical roots of data storage and retrieval. This is "insurance data," the first category of data created by the Digital Revolution. And while insurance is great, its drawbacks are obvious: A disaster must strike before you can cash in on the policy.

The reasons for data retrieval are many, but all too often it entails: retrieving a file for an anxious or angry someone who has lost or destroyed it; rebuilding data infrastructure following a disaster, while being told that the clock is ticking and your organization may not survive if the data is not recovered quickly enough; or helping an antagonist find incriminating evidence against someone in e-discovery. No wonder organization heads like to have data deleted at the earliest possible moment. As important as it is, data storage is often seen as a real liability. There is logic to this position. Some data qualifies for Sydney

Brenner's definition of "garbage" and should be removed before it begins to smell.

Insurance data is not going away any time soon. In fact, thanks to the Digital Revolution, even more of it is being generated. However, a growing amount of digital information now being created does not fall into the category of backups, disaster recovery copies, or stagnant, legally mandated archives. Organizations are now looking at data not as a single, monolithic blob, but as a diverse collection of information with varied potential that, in turn, has different requirements for storage and protection. A great movement within the Digital Revolution is the monetization of information, a trend that reflects a value in data sets not previously recognized.

Unlike insurance data that is used to recreate the past, much of the information being created today can be used to predict the future. Capturing and storing consumer buyer behavior provides insight into future buying patterns, the understanding of which can lead to better products, easier customer purchasing options, and lower costs. Chapter 4 more closely examines the predictive value of data.

Another field generating large amounts of data is genomic research. Mapping the human genome allows for custom medical treatments and new medical techniques that are saving and prolonging lives. In some instances, it is now possible to predict which medications certain individuals will best respond to based solely on their genome map.

These are but two examples of the digital world exploding around us, with data helping us build a reality that is more fantastic than even science-fiction writers can imagine. This is "value data," the second type of data created by digital technology. Value data does not change once it is created or captured, and there is no need to back it up again and again. However, because of its value—and because it is oftentimes data that cannot be recreated at a later point in time—it should be kept secure for a very long period, perhaps indefinitely, to be retrieved whenever it is needed, whether a week, a year, or a decade later or longer.

Preserving the Organizational Genome

Understanding the distinction between insurance data and value data allows organizations to better evaluate how each type of data should be protected. Many organizations are using the same data protection process for both data types. This book suggests that existing backup methods may be sufficient for daily backups of insurance data but not sufficient for the digital preservation of value data.

All too often the goal is simply to copy or replicate the data to a second area and call it good. Because insurance data is rarely if ever accessed again, and because there are multiple copies of every file, testing a system's ability to retrieve the data is rarely a high priority, especially since this area is just one of the many areas that IT professionals manage in addition to rolling out new applications, keeping networks up and running, managing tier-1 storage, troubleshooting individual systems, and executing other day-to-day, higher-profile tasks. IT will get a call immediately if a server is not available, a mission-critical application is not responding, or when the website is down. No one ever calls in the morning to say, "Hey! Great backup last night!" If backups work well, no one other than the backup administrator knows about it.

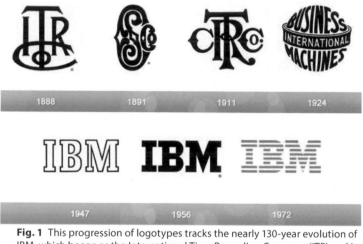

Fig. 1 This progression of logotypes tracks the nearly 130-year evolution of IBM, which began as the International Time Recording Company (ITR) and is today one of the world's oldest corporate genomes.

Most important, backup and disaster recovery plans are not always real-world tested for their true restoration capabilities, or they are tested initially and then not retested after many aspects of the IT infrastructure have changed. According to research by the information management company Iron Mountain, 32 percent of IT administrators surveyed said they do not do regular testing of their backup systems.[6]

This alarming statistic underscores the importance of reconsidering the current methods that are being used to protect information being created. Although it might involve much of the same equipment and procedures, the task of digital preservation is a far different one than a traditional IT backup. Properly considered, digital preservation does not apply to all information and nor does it replace the need for traditional IT backup. It should instead be viewed as a separate activity focused on long-term retrieval capability and absolute data integrity. In this regard, the consideration of formats, metadata, and media is much more important than it is with traditional storage tasks. Will a particular format of data be readable in one decade, several decades, or tens of decades? This is a critical question and only one of many being raised in the world of digital preservation. Later chapters of this book will revisit this question and other concerns, such as how to hedge against threats by using multiple types of media when creating copies. In short, the best answer is genetic diversity.

This chapter has only presented a glimpse of the potential value that new types of data have for organizations in general. However, the value of information generated today varies substantially depending on the individual organization examined, or the vertical market or market segment to which it belongs. Chapter 4 provides a closer look at how organizations can be categorized or grouped by how they create, capture, and utilize information.

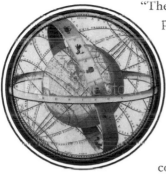

"The ancient Babylonians became extremely adept at predicting the timing of astronomical events…They accumulated centuries of accurate observations, noted regularities (periodicities) in the behaviors, and extrapolated those regularities into the future. In other words, they assumed that future cycles of behavior in the celestial realm would reproduce past behavior, as it had been observed to do repeatedly in the past. 'Big data' is all the rage today, but the basic concept goes back a long way, for it is none other than the method of ancient Babylonian astronomy."

—Frank Wilczek, *A Beautiful Question: Finding Nature's Deep Design*

Chapter 4

The Value of Information

For the past several years, the topics of Big Data and data analytics have dominated technology conversations. Both terms refer to the approach of using data gathered in the past to forecast a future outcome, and as tools they can be applied to many types of data, whether global, as with worldwide weather, or company specific, as with the expected life of a manufactured component. Name it, however, and data analytics can probably be used to forecast it—from where to find oil deposits to which street intersection needs a traffic signal instead of a stop sign to even how to optimize an election campaign.

As the Wilczek quotation opening this chapter indicates, data analytics are not new; the basic concept has been around for millennia. What is new are some of the *applications* of data analytics. Big Data refers to analytics with less-structured, "fuzzier" data sets. Traditional analytics, using On-Line Application Processing (OLAP), expects highly typed, structured data, such as a corporation's financial data or sales records. Big Data is used to find statistical relationships between these sources and less orderly sources, including search queries, weather patterns, or website visits—truly, any data set that researchers can get their hands on. Big Data is less about structure and sparsity than it is about choosing plentiful input data over precision.

This more evolved approach to utilizing data illustrates a trend in data creation and retention: the rise of unstructured data. Tidy, structured data that fits into orderly rows in indexed tables is by nature limited by the effort required to groom and categorize it. The Big Data model encourages the creation and retention of far more data. Search queries or posts on Facebook are less structured than financial data. Seismic data or cat videos on YouTube exhibit even less structure. A detailed look at data creation and data retention suggests that structured data is growing linearly, while the exponential growth explosion is in unstructured data.[1]

More and more businesses are using data analytics to predict buyer behavior, and this is influencing their business decisions. The Intelligence Unit of *The Economist* conducted a 2012 survey of more than 600 executives from various international markets to better understand the impact of data analytics on their operations. Over half of those surveyed said that management decisions based purely on intuition or experience—traits valued highly in the past—are being increasingly considered suspect. The Intelligence Unit reported that, on average, survey participants believed that Big Data had increased organizational performance by 26 percent in the previous three years, and that they also believed it would improve performance by an average of 41 percent in the subsequent three years."[2]

Several high-profile examples illustrate how this is playing out. As a staff writer for *The New York Times*, author and journalist Charles Duhigg wrote an insightful piece on how retailer Target used data analytics to market to pregnant women. Why specifically pregnant women? Buying habits are hard to break, but there are a few life events that tend to break down existing habits. Having a new baby is one of them. The first challenge that Target faced was to figure out which of its female customers were pregnant. A data statistician at Target revealed to Duhigg that Target "was able to identify about 25 products that, when analyzed together, allowed him to assign to each shopper a 'pregnancy prediction' score. More important, he could also estimate her due date to within a small window, so Target could send coupons timed to very specific stages of her pregnancy."[3] This is an amazing amount of information to predict from cash register receipts alone!

It was not merely the list of products purchased that signaled pregnancy. Just as important were changes in products purchased and the timing of these changes. Lotion and soap were two of the products examined. The most important indicator was when customers changed the type of soap and lotion they were purchasing. When women switched from perfumed to unscented lotion or soap, their pregnancy prediction score increased, illustrating a very important point about data analytics: The more history you have, the more accurate your predictions become. If you have no history on a customer who walks into your store and buys unscented soap or lotion, their purchase tells you very little. It was the ability to detect a change in behavior that allowed Target to identify a key customer demographic. Without this additional data, records of new purchases would have been useless.

This marketing anecdote raises an important caveat, however. As organizations find new ways to improve business practices through the use of analytics, they must also recognize the ethical responsibilities that come with it. Many consumers would find some forms of data mining inappropriate. For instance, when the above Target example was made public, it was quite controversial and created negative publicity for the retailer. As with many new technologies, a balance must be struck between insight and intrusiveness.

The Six Data User Archetypes

As organizations move from having to save information to wanting to save information, the question arises: Just what type of data collectors are they? Data collection can be categorized as performed by six major types of users. These are not exclusive categories, since most organizations represent a combination of types. They are:

- Data decision-makers
- Data creators
- Data explorers
- Data brokers
- Data curators
- Data scientists

Data decision-makers

The first question that IT professionals must ask themselves is, "What information should I keep and what should I delete?" With more and more business intelligence being extracted from seemingly inconsequential data, IT professionals are regularly requested to keep everything "forever," a daunting task.

The work of data decision-makers fits into the existing category of general IT because organizations must first better understand their existing customer history. The same can be said of information concerning their employees, manufacturing processes, human resources policies, and so forth. General IT is the holder of all internal data for an organization and can therefore play a leading role in leveraging the Digital Revolution, which, if it has disrupted anything at all, has disrupted business decision-making. As Gartner, a top industry analyst firm, recently concluded, "IT is no longer just about the IT function. Instead, IT has become the catalyst for the next phase of innovation in personal and competitive business ecosystems."[24]

As data gathered from daily operations increasingly becomes a top corporate asset, more and more companies are evaluating ways to preserve data that was once considered expendable. In fact, an emerging role for data managers in many organizations is that of chief data officer, or CDO. In its recent research, Gartner predicts that by 2017 half of all companies in regulated and compliance-heavy businesses will have a CDO.[5]

Data creators

Data decision-makers deal with the data collected from existing interactions with customers and other business operations. The creation of new information is not the main purpose of their operations, but rather is an aftereffect of individual business transactions. Several fields deal with data creation quite differently. Of them, the broad field of media and entertainment (M&E) is an excellent example of data creation being the main product of the business itself.

When thinking of M&E as a vertical market, what might quickly come to mind are large movie houses like Warner Bros. or 21st Century Fox. Organizations like these certainly create a great deal of digital information each time they release a feature film, but they are far from the only organizations in the M&E market. Major professional sports teams produce digital content when they record their games, which may be broadcast live, rebroadcast later, made available in small clips for news reporting over the current season, or used in subsequent decades for a player retrospective or to commemorate a sports anniversary.

Other data creators belonging to this vertical market include major houses of worship that broadcast their sermons. Much like sports organizations do, they may package parts or the whole of a broadcast for later playback. News organizations retain footage of politicians, celebrities, and major news events. Large corporations create videos for internal training, product descriptions, and employee recruitment. Even universities function as media houses when they record their own sporting events, create teaching materials, and recruit students.

All in all, this is a very broad group of data users and creators. However, there are two main differences between the M&E vertical market and general IT. First, as indicated above, the digital asset created by an M&E group is often the product in and of itself and the key component of revenue generation. This is the "monetization" of data in action, and the value of this data can continue indefinitely. The movie *Gone With the Wind* was released in 1939, yet it continues to be played and re-released in new digitization or improved color versions. While it is easy to predict that a blockbuster film will retain value far into the future, many other assets can prove surprisingly valuable long after their initial creation.

Take the case of Michael Jackson, who started his career as a world-famous entertainer at age five. By the age of 49, Jackson was plagued by legal troubles and the accusations of unethical activities that limited his appeal, and so footage from his early days was not in high demand and had little value. But when the singer died unexpectedly a year later, just before he was scheduled to perform in a sold-out series of comeback concerts in London, any and all footage of Jackson was immediately in high demand. Every major television station around the world ran exposés on the singer's life within hours of his death. A recording of the Jackson Five performing on *The Ed Sullivan Show* 45 years earlier was suddenly of great financial value. In 2010, Zack O'Malley Greenburg wrote for *Forbes* that:

> Fueled by a bonanza of interest following Jackson's death, his estate raked in $275 million over the past 12 months, by our estimates. That's more than enough to earn the King of Pop the top spot on our annual Dead Celebs list; in fact, it's more than the rest of the artists on the list put together, and more than any living artist or group.[6]

The lesson is clear. Virtually all digital assets created in the M&E vertical market should be treated as products with both current and future value, monetized and expected to be held indefinitely—a sharp contrast to organizations that retain data for compliance mandates, for which data will typically have little to no value once the retention period of the mandate is reached.

Another way in which M&E data differs from general IT data relates to this "data-as-product" categorization. Files and databases captured by general IT are in constant flux, accessed and changed, sometimes hourly, with no way of knowing when or how the data will be accessed or manipulated by users. For example, the output of a training video, news event, movie, sports game, or sermon is at some point considered "finished." The original data source is not constantly accessed once its initial purpose is served. Rather than running constant daily incremental backups and weekly full backups on these digital assets, organizations tend to archive them for long-term holding.

Such an archive is often referred to as the "golden archive," since it is a singular copy of digital information that, once stored, is not available online. It must first be located and restored to an access point. Historically, these assets have been archived to tape, much like general IT data. Unlike general IT data, however, they are more likely to be stored in closely monitored, climate-controlled environments. (The greater the recognized value of data, the better its care tends to be.) As the industry moves from the traditional approach of simply copying data toward true digital preservation—that is, both storing data and bringing it back— the archival process itself becomes more important. Data creators of this vertical market have pioneered proper archiving and have much to teach any organization hoping to hold information indefinitely.

Data explorers

While most organizations use data for discovery, the title data explorers best describes those in the high-performance computing (HPC) industry. The world of HPC relies on supercomputers that "play an important role in the field of computational science, and are used for a wide range of computationally intensive tasks in various fields, including quantum mechanics, weather forecasting, climate research, oil and gas exploration, molecular modeling, and  physical simulations (such as simulations of the early moments of the universe, airplane and spacecraft aerodynamics, the detonation of nuclear weapons, and nuclear fusion)."[7]

How does HPC work? First, computational test scenarios manipulate a digital environment or situation. Data is then run through these test scenarios and the output of the tests or experiments is collected. The computational capability of these systems is staggering, with their performance measured in the number of floating point operations per second, referred to as FLOPS. Two examples of floating point operations are 1.2345 x 678.9 and 5 x π (to the precision of the processor). At the time of this writing, a system must have a minimum performance of 20 teraflops—the ability to calculate 20 trillion equations per second—to qualify as one of the top 500 supercomputers in existence. As of November 2015, the fastest supercomputer in the world was China's supercomputer Tianhe-2, which can compute at over 33 petaflops, or over 33 quadrillion operations per second![8]

One well-known supercomputing site is the European Organization for Nuclear Research (CERN). Although it does not operate the largest supercomputer, CERN is the largest particle physics laboratory in the world and home to the Large Hadron Collider (LHC), the world's largest and most powerful particle collider (Figure 1). The LHC was thought to be powerful enough to confirm the existence of the Higgs boson, or Higgs particle.

The Higgs boson is sometimes referred to as the "God particle" due to its theoretical ability to provide mass to all other particles and so create the gravitational force that holds the universe together. Its existence was finally confirmed through the analysis of two years' worth of data collected by the massive ATLAS and CMS experiments that used the LHC. François Englert and Peter W. Higgs subsequently shared the 2013 Nobel Prize in Physics for their 1964 papers that laid out the theory that predicted the particle's existence.

Fig. 1 CERN's Large Hadron Collider is essentially a 27-kilometer (~17-mile) ring of superconducting magnets lying 100 meters (328 feet) underground.

This illustrates the challenge facing any experimental computing facility: Experiments are often repeated and reexamined. All inputs and outputs—that is, all the digital data related to a project—must be preserved. At what point in history will we decide that we no longer need the experimental output that proved the existence of the God particle? If that data were lost and had to be reproduced, the cost would be staggering given that the total expense of finding the Higgs boson is estimated at more than $13 billion dollars.[9]

In 2013, CERN announced that it had recorded over 100 petabytes of data over the past 20 years.[10] Interestingly enough, experiments with the LHC from just the past three years are responsible for 75 of those 100 petabytes. As is being seen in all types of organizations, the data being created using HPC is increasing at an exponential rate.

The difference between the world of the HPC data explorers and the vertical markets previously discussed is largely one of scale. Even at the digital size of high definition, full-length movies cannot compare: The output of a single experiment dwarfs the amount of data contained in hundreds of movies. HPC sites rival data repositories of any vertical market and are probably second in size only to Internet operations, the next vertical market discussed in this chapter.

Although data sets are regularly shared among engineers, scientists, and developers who work in the HPC world, their workflows are more "manual" than those of general IT. Once the output of an experiment or modeling session is done, it does not change, and so it can be moved to a data repository requiring lower access and hopefully offering much greater density and energy efficiency for storage.

One of the first commercial applications for HPC was seismic exploration for minerals and petroleum. What ultrasound is to doctors, seismic vibrations are to oil drillers. Seismic exploration measures the spread of waves through the earth. By measuring speed, reflection, and refraction on or near the earth's surface, data explorers can predict material composition deep underground. This tool has been used for mineral exploration for decades, but it was far less effective before the invention of high-performance computing that could generate—and analyze—the tremendous amounts of data required for efficacy.

Thanks to HPC, the era of drilling to determine what were dry wells and what were gushers is now as dated as the black-and-white footage that documents it. Advances in HPC and data analysis have all but eliminated the ambiguity of finding oil, and horizontal drilling enables drillers to physically access oil once data explorers have located it with precision.

The important point to note here, however, is that although technologies for reaching and extracting oil and natural gas deposits have evolved, they still rely on seismic information gathered decades ago on deposits that were unreachable at the time. Geologists therefore have not had to spend millions of dollars to resurvey and perform new seismic explorations. No matter its age, geological data remains as good today as it was on the day it was first recorded and can be reanalyzed using the latest and most accurate methods. It is not a surprise then that most data explorers using HPC view the output of their operations as valuable data requiring indefinite preservation.

In this respect they are not alone. At the end of 2015, CERN was preparing to enter "season two" of LHC computing and has projected that they will need 140 petabytes of storage—a millennium's worth of full HD-quality movies![11] The needs of data explorers are creating a demand for storage that only one other data user can match—the data broker.

Data brokers

Unlike the organizations that both produce and distribute digital assets, data brokers collect and repackage information for subsequent access or distribution. This is one of the fastest growing areas in terms of data growth and unstructured data. Most Internet companies can be categorized as data brokers.

Internet search-engine companies are the most visible data brokers and include, among others, Google, Baidu, Bing, Yahoo, and Ask.com. These firms have documented everything that their customers have looked up online and may even know more about us than our closest friends and family members do. Recall the last time you planned a vacation. Your friends might have known your ultimate destination, but the search engine you used also knows the other places you considered, as well as the exact details of the hotel and rental car you chose.

Social media sites like Facebook, LinkedIn, Twitter, and YouTube also fall into the data broker category, although their approach differs from that of Internet search engines in that the data they collect comes not from your browsing history, but directly from you. Every post you like and every person you friend tells Facebook what and who you like. If you are impressed with someone's abilities, you can endorse them on LinkedIn. Similarly, if you are impressed with your own abilities, you can upload your resume and share the same professional goals you hold with other LinkedIn users—and with LinkedIn itself. YouTube knows what you like to watch most, and Twitter knows what you most like to talk about.

The power of such data is uncanny. Stanford Graduate School of Business research suggests that "a computer needs the data from only 10 Facebook 'likes' to beat the accuracy of a person's coworker at judging his or her personality traits, such as extraversion, conscientiousness, and neuroticism. The computer needs 70 'likes' to be more accurate than a person's friends. With 250 Facebook data points, the computer can beat someone's spouse."[12]

The staggering amount of information involved in all of this is evident in the six billion collective hours of videos watched on YouTube every month and the other billion videos watched on mobile phones every day.[13] LinkedIn has more than 300 million users and adds two members to its fold every second.[14] According to a white paper published by Facebook in late 2013, its users share an average of 4.7 content items with other users and upload 350 million photos every day. At the time that the paper was written, Facebook boasted storing more than 250 petabytes of information and taking in another half a petabyte every day.[15] To wrap your brain around just how much information this is, consider the following representations of only one petabyte of information:[16]

- If the average MP3 encoding rate for mobile is approximately one megabyte per minute, and if the average song is about four minutes long, it would take more than 2,000 years to play a petabyte's worth of songs.
- If a smartphone camera photo three megabytes in size were printed at 8.5 inches wide, then one petabyte of printed photos laid side by side would stretch more than 48,000 miles—nearly enough to wrap around the equator twice.
- If you counted all the bits in one petabyte at a rate of one bit per second, you would be counting for 285 million years.

The public willingly provides vast amounts of information to data brokers in exchange for free services. Data brokers know likes, dislikes, wish lists, dream vacations, favorite cars, and preferred appliances. They know ages, genders, locations, and spending habits. The customers whom these organizations are serving are also in turn the "products" being sold. According to the online publication *Small Business Trends,* Facebook has more than one million small- or medium-sized businesses as advertisers and large companies are spending as much as $100 million on Facebook advertising annually. It also reported that Twitter charges an estimated $200,000 for a 24-hour promoted trend, and YouTube, a free service, is "expected to generate $5.6 billion in 2016."[17]

Other types of data brokers include Internet-based companies that store photos, such as SmugMug, Snapfish, and flickr, which provide users with an easy way to store and share photos, print them, or use them to create customized calendars, coffee mugs, or greeting cards. Cloud storage providers fit into this group as well: Amazon Web Services, Google Cloud Storage, and Microsoft Azure provide data management, storage, and restoration to businesses for a fee. All provide personal storage for little or no money as part of a suite of products that is funded by data collection and advertisement revenues.

Many organizations monetize data, meaning that their data is their product. Data brokers take this one step further: Their data is their company, and they would cease to exist if they lost it all. These data brokers represent the largest data repositories on earth. Although few of them will disclose exactly how much data they are working with, it is estimated that some have exceeded petabytes and now hold upwards of an exabyte—or 1,024 petabytes. Protecting this vast wealth of data is one of the greatest tests facing these organizations.

Data curators

The home of the next type of data-driven organization may surprise you. Imagine walking down a long peaceful corridor, which ends at the entrance of a round room with marble floors and marble columns. It is very quiet and you are surrounded by bronze statues and beautiful antique oaken desks. Above you is a domed ceiling that is stunning beyond description. This is the main reading room of a data curator, the Library of Congress (LOC), the largest library in the world with more than 162 million items in its collection. What a refreshing change from exabytes and petabytes! But if you cannot visit the library in person, do not fear: A quick Google search allows you to see its contents for yourself.

Data curators fall into a category all their own. The LOC is joined by other national libraries, state archives, and public and private museums worldwide in belonging to the network known as the International Internet Preservation Consortium (IIPC), made up of experts who are committed to archiving the Web. Established by the LOC in 2000, the consortium was joined by the national libraries of Australia, Canada, Denmark, Finland, France, Iceland, Italy, Norway, Sweden, Great Britain, as well as the Internet Archive (three years later). By March 2014 the IIPC had expanded to 48 separate member organizations. Even the Digital Revolution itself is being digitally archived.

Data curators do not create or manipulate data. They instead collect, preserve, and organize it so that it is available to everyone for all time. Although a great deal of the data they offer is available online, most of it is not. These "brick and mortar" organizations also tend to focus more on the originals than on reproduced digital copies, which are much easier to view from afar. Nevertheless, as holders of vast amounts of digital content they are setting standards for the new practice of digital preservation, the process whereby the accessibility and readability of digital information is maintained for as long as is necessary, regardless of storage device failure or changes in technology.

Their efforts combined, data curators put petabytes of data online and into storage. For data curators, preservation is the top priority and digital content is seen as one more way of ensuring that information persists. This is one of the few groups that really means "forever" when discussing data retention policies. They also host many of the projects that exemplify this movement, including the National Digital Stewardship Alliance, the Digital Preservation Outreach and Education Program, and the National Digital Information Infrastructure and Preservation Program.

Fig. 2 A legacy reborn. The Bibliotheca Alexandrina in Alexandria, Egypt, is dedicated to the spirit of openness, scholarship, and cultural advancement.

Of the world's data curators, the LOC is perhaps one of the best representatives of its category, since it is not out of theory but out of experience that has led it to become a leader in digital stewardship and preservation, having once suffered great damage from invading British armies in 1814, as well as a massive fire in 1851 that destroyed nearly two-thirds of its books. One cannot help but see the parallel that exists in the irreparable loss suffered by yet another magnificent library—the Royal Library of Alexandria, which existed from roughly 300 BCE to 370 CE, and was arguably one the most significant libraries and centers of scholarship of its time. Over the centuries, however, multiple fires and attacks eventually left its buildings in ruins and its fragile scrolls destroyed. The loss of the library is considered the archetypal symbol of lost knowledge and is an ancient example to be well heeded even today.

Many individuals might have trouble drawing connections between the activities of data curators and the operations of their own organizations, but it is important to recognize that these groups have spent more time and effort on examining the preservation of information than any other data-use groups described in this chapter. An organization that is seriously dedicated to preserving its information, for whatever reason, could do far worse than be guided by the research and proposals shared by groups such as the National Digital Stewardship Alliance.

Data scientists

The final category of data users, data scientists, overlaps with the category of data explorers and high-performance computing. Data scientists are carved out as a separate subcategory to show how many of the technologies that we work with today have an interesting past and an extraordinary future thanks to the Digital Revolution.

Archetypal examples of data scientists are the groups that work in bioscience—medical and genomic research—and in astronomy. What these seemingly very different groups have in common is that they use data to examine extant phenomena invisible to the naked eye. Data scientists "look at" everything from cells and cell processes in the human body, DNA, and genomes to galaxies, black holes, and atomic particles.

The highly sophisticated technologies used in bioscience today were built upon technological achievements and innovations that unfolded across centuries. Technological progress, while astounding, took place on a long, incremental timeline. An excellent example of this is the development of the thermometer. First introduced by Galileo in 1592, it originally had no scale and was only useful in showing rising and falling temperatures. Around 1600, a scale was introduced to the thermometer. Roughly a century later, Gabriel Fahrenheit introduced the use of mercury as a more predictable expansion medium. Another 50 years passed and, in 1742, Anders Celsius developed the Celsius scale we use today, with zero as water's freezing point and 100 as its boiling point. Yet it was not until 1868 that Carl Wunderlich studied the body heat of more than 2,500 patients, establishing a normal temperature range for healthy individuals. All told, more than 275 years had to pass before the thermometer became a useful tool in medical practice. Likewise, the microscope, first created in the late 1500s, did not come into medical use until after two centuries' worth of improvements.

In stark contrast, modern technological progress has increased the speed of progress itself; in the past century we have seen a far more rapid rate of both technological innovation and adoption. The introduction of the computer to the medical industry revolutionized medical care and research, with computers becoming central to the delivery of medical care by the 1950s. Faster computers made possible the development of imaging techniques, such as magnetic resonance imaging (MRI) and positron emission tomography (PET). Basic medical diagnostic tools—X-rays, CT scans, nuclear medicine scans, ultrasound, mammography, and fluoroscopy—and countless others have become digitized, with the records they create likely to be kept and tracked for a patient's entire life. In any medical research involving patients, it is expected that data will be kept even beyond a subject's lifetime. The marketing research firm MarketsandMarkets estimates that "globally, medical image archives are increasing by 20 percent to 40 percent each year."[18]

A model put out by the consulting firm Frost & Sullivan projects that "even if diagnostic imaging volumes plateau around the 600 million procedures per year mark, overall storage and archiving volume requirements for U.S. medical imaging data will cross the one-exabyte mark by 2016."[19] Despite this staggering amount of data, medical imaging is only one area of bioscience data creation. Another major contribution to data accumulation in the data scientist category comes from genome sequencing.

If medical images are designed to serve individuals, then genome sequencing serves all of humankind. The Human Genome Project, led by the National Institutes of Health (NIH), was completed in 2003. The reference genome that it produced has fundamentally transformed not only the field of genetics, but also the fields of medicine, zoology, and anthropology. We have come a long way since Gregor Mendel presented his laws of heredity in 1865, yet that was the beginning of the trail that has led us to genome sequencing.

The well-known cofounder of Apple Computers, Steve Jobs, was among the first 20 people in the world to have his DNA sequenced. He also had the DNA of his cancer sequenced. At the time, it cost roughly $100,000.[20] The drop in price for individual genome sequencing since then has even outpaced the drop in price that would be predicted by Moore's Law (Figure 3). The National Human Genome Research Institute (NHGRI) reports that prices for a complete individual genome sequence are now as low as $1,000. With lower prices comes higher demand. Scientists are expecting as many as one billion people to have their genomes sequenced by 2025.[21] Genome sequencing now allows us to:

- understand how the same type of cancer can present differently in different patients and adopt a treatment regime specific to each individual;
- compare the genomes of different types of plants and animals to gain invaluable insight into biology and evolution; and
- study and identify the causes of rare genetic diseases.

As with many sciences, genomic research has called for more computing power and more storage for the information created. The *PLOS Biology* study, "Big Data: Astronomical or Genomical?" predicts that genome sequencing will soon take the lead as the largest generator of data worldwide.[22] Based on current growth rates, which double every seven months, the study predicts that DNA sequencing will approach one zettabyte of outputted data per year by 2025, which would eclipse even YouTube's data creation, projected at one to two exabytes per year by 2025.[23] Each human genome sequence requires roughly 600 gigabytes of storage. Once collected, this data can provide valuable information not only for individuals, but also for their descendants. For this reason, there is no expiration date for genomic data.

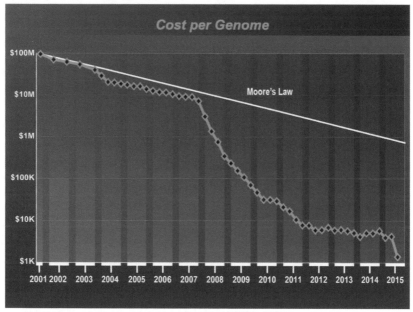

Fig. 3 The cost of genomic sequencing from 2001 to 2015.

It is easy to see the medical benefits of genome sequencing. The NIH and NHGRI are now turning their attention to how genome sequencing can be used to benefit society at large. According to the NHGRI's *Blueprint for the Genomic Era*, they will "now address research that focuses on society itself, more than on biology or health. Such efforts should enable the research community to analyze the impact of genomics on concepts of race, ethnicity, kinship, individual and group identity, health, disease and 'normality' for traits and behaviors."[24]

As these data scientists look inward, other data scientists are looking upward. As with medical science, astronomy is a discipline with a long pedigree. The history of the telescope can be traced back to 3500 BCE, when the Phoenicians discovered glass by cooking on sand. It would be another 5,000 years before this invention was turned toward the stars. In 1608, a German-Dutch spectacle-maker, Hans Lippershey, discovered that he could bring objects closer in view by holding two lenses some distance apart. Although his patent on the invention was denied, this is the first documented creation of a telescope.

Today's great innovation in astronomy has been to combine optics with scientific instruments and spacecraft systems. A well-known and highly successful example is the Hubble Space Telescope, an invention that has opened up a window to the universe once unimaginable to previous generations. According to the Space Telescope Science Institute, in the two decades that it has orbited the earth:

> Hubble has helped to answer some of the most compelling astronomical questions of our time—and uncovered mysteries we never knew existed. Investigating everything from black holes to planets around other stars, Hubble has changed the face of astronomy, ushering in a new chapter of humanity's exploration of the universe.[25]

While Hubble in space and other high-powered, land-based telescopes digitize images and create massive amounts of data, the greatest challenges from the perspective of data preservation will come from future telescopes. And that future is very much based on radio telescopes, the best known of which is the Arecibo Observatory in Puerto Rico, made famous by the science-fiction drama *Contact.*

Radio astronomy is not limited by weather, so cloudy skies are not a problem, and thanks to the use of longer wavelengths, radio telescopes can even "see" areas of space obscured by cosmic dust. The basics of this technology have been in use since the 1930s, but scientists and engineers are now using it to create radio devices on a scale never seen before.

The Square Kilometre Array (SKA), phase one of which is scheduled for completion in 2023,[26] will be the world's largest radio telescope. Whereas the Arecibo Observatory uses a single dish, the full SKA will be located in the Southern Hemisphere in sub-Saharan areas to ensure the least radio interference and the best view of the Milky Way Galaxy. The name SKA refers to the original goal of building a telescope with a "collecting area" of one square kilometer (although the dishes and antennas used to do this will in fact be distributed over a much larger area). The SKA will include between several hundred to upwards of two thousand parabolic dishes, each measuring 15 meters [about 50 feet] in diameter. Most of the dishes will be sited in South Africa, with others located in SKA African partner countries. Australia is a second major location for the SKA effort, where a large number of telescopes that are being used as a test-bed for the SKA project have been installed. There will also be more than 100,000 antennas located at the site, with a planned increase to one million antennas in phase two of the project, expected to be completed in the late 2020s.

In total, the raw data that these antennas will eventually generate is projected to be roughly 10 times the amount of data generated by all Internet traffic worldwide.[27] Each telescope will analyze one exabyte of data per day.[28] The good news: This technology deploys significant data reduction. Incoming data is reduced by as much as 10,000 times before being recorded. The challenging news: The final data sets that make it to archive will still account for multiple petabytes per year. The estimated five-year output to archive is on the scale of one exabyte, and by the completion of phase two, the telescope will have an estimated 10 times the antennas and may have 100 times the data,[29] which will be made available to scientists worldwide and likely be examined many times over. The SKA Organization describes the goals of the SKA projects as such:

> The SKA will be used to answer fundamental questions of science and about the laws of nature, such as: How did the universe, and the stars and galaxies contained in it, form and evolve? Was Einstein's theory of relativity correct? What is the nature of "dark matter" and "dark energy"? What is the origin of cosmic magnetism? Is there life somewhere else in the universe? But, perhaps, the most significant discoveries to be made by the SKA are those we cannot predict.[30]

This leads to a question that hangs over all of the data categories discussed in this chapter: When is it acceptable to delete the information that has been created by projects, products, and industries? Perhaps the question should be restated: What is the expiration date for data sets that help us understand the universe? When will the output from an experiment that identified the "God particle" no longer be of interest or value? Will there be a time when the original writings of a country's founders are no longer needed? Less dramatic, will there be a time when we need no longer strengthen our businesses through investigative analytics? Will there come a day when we no longer think classic movies—or even pictures of loved ones—should be preserved?

Both human survival and progress now rely heavily on computing power and the data sets created through art, science, and commerce. Destruction or loss of that data would set humankind back substantially. The remaining chapters of this book are dedicated to examining threats to information, the technology available for preserving this information, and the ways in which we can leverage technologies to protect that most precious of archives: society's genome.

Fig. 4 and Fig. 5 *(Left)* The SKA project involves installing hundreds, eventually thousands, of mid- to high-frequency dishes in South Africa and elsewhere in Africa and *(right)* hundreds of thousands to one million low-frequency antennas in Western Australia.

"Many civilizations in history were destroyed by the simple technologies of fire and the sword. Indeed, of all civilizations in history, the overwhelming majority have been destroyed, some intentionally, some as a result of plague or natural disaster. Virtually all of them could have avoided the catastrophes that destroyed them if only they had possessed a little additional knowledge, such as improved agricultural or military technology, better hygiene, or better political or economic institutions. Very few, if any, could have been saved by greater caution about innovation."

—David Deustch, *The Beginning of Infinity: Explanations That Transform the World*

Chapter 5

Incidents, Accidents, and Disasters

Like it or not, data disasters occur every day, although not necessarily where you live and work. They often happen when least expected and adversely affect an organization long before anyone recognizes what has transpired. Data destruction, accidental or intentional, will happen. It is a fact of digital life.

A 2013 *Forbes* magazine article by J. P. Blaho, an IT consultant for the data recovery company Sungard Availability Services, outlined how IT staff should broach the topic of disaster preparation and recovery with management. Blaho encourages staffers to avoid using the word "disaster" when dealing with executives and upper management. "You'll lose their attention and bore them," he cautions. Instead, he suggests using more appealing terms, such as "value proposition" and "return on investment."[1] As Blaho notes, the challenge facing IT professionals is that most senior-management personnel believe that they have already successfully addressed their disaster-related issues when, in fact, it is simply not enough to have backup and recovery software in place.

It is no surprise then that the critical importance of data becomes especially apparent during—and after—periods of adversity, such as with high-profile events like a flood, fire, or terrorist attack. Nevertheless, it is worth taking a closer look at some of the ongoing issues that individuals and enterprise IT systems are facing in today's digital environment.

The possible causes of breach and loss are legion, but a few stand out for their capacity to inflict damage—and IT does not need to look beyond the doors of its own organization to find them. According to research by cyber-security provider Symantec, well-intentioned employees and general IT errors account for about two-thirds of all data breaches. More often than not, a catastrophe results from an innocent, unintended act, such as a database administrator accidentally eradicating all copies of a data archive.

Fig. 1 USB flash drives have write-protector switches to stop a virus, malware, Trojan, or other infection.

Whatever the cause, data breaches are costly.

On average, a compromised record costs an organization around $200; a lost laptop, about $50,000.[2] Small and mid-sized businesses lose roughly $70,000 for every hour of digital downtime.[3] In 2012, data breaches cost the average company more than $5 million,[4] making it is easy to see why many enterprises never recover from a serious data loss.

Setting statistics aside to take a critical view of the situation, security starts with ascertaining whether everyone who uses IT resources—from regular employees to top-level executives—is receiving ongoing education regarding trending digital hazards, since external threats are ever present and cybercriminals are constantly changing their modes of operation, as well as the look and feel of their stings.

Spear phishing, for example, is an excellent example of a sophisticated cybercrime. An e-mail message received on a company PC will look completely legitimate. Written with savvy, its content will appear appropriate and its topic germane to the employee who receives it. But a click of a single link in the message can unleash a malware attack against not only the employee's computer, but against the computers of his company, customers, and vendors. An organization that allows the use of employee-owned thumb drives on corporate computers or that lacks prudent "bring your own device" (BYOD) security policies is particularly vulnerable. There are few better ways to propagate malware than by directly inviting hackers into your offices and data centers.

Unfortunately, the risks for data loss are growing at a time when IT resources are shrinking. Budget cuts, reduced staff, and outsourcing during an unprecedented period of mounting malware threats can challenge even the best, most experienced IT support staff. Nevertheless, the consequences of losing any battle against PC incidents, accidents, and disasters grow greater every day and cannot be ignored.

Natural Disasters: The Sandy Effect

Compared to IT glitches and employee errors, events such as fires, floods, and extreme weather actually account for a relatively small portion of IT damage and data loss. Nevertheless, any meaningful plan for long-term data preservation must account for the threat posed by these and other natural disasters. These events are rare (and referred to as "high beta"—a measure of volatility), but the catastrophic nature of their potential damage requires solutions that are not only robust, but also economical and practical.

Consider the case of Hurricane Sandy, the epic 2012 storm that swept through the Caribbean and up the East Coast, leaving death and destruction in its wake. The cost in the loss of human lives alone was devastating, and the damage to infrastructures, homes, and the environment was long-lasting and profound.

Hurricane Sandy occurred seven years after the even more powerful Hurricane Katrina, and more than a decade after the tragic events of 9/11. Had America's IT professionals been prepared for Sandy by having learned from history? Apparently not enough. A full moon had increased high tides and Sandy surged substantially when it made landfall in the United States near Atlantic City, New Jersey, as a post-tropical cyclone with hurricane-force winds. Electricity failed throughout the New York–New Jersey area on a level that New York City's electric utility company, Con Edison, called "the largest storm-related outage in our history."[5]

Fig. 2 NYC's flooded South Ferry subway station shows how severely Hurricane Sandy impacted basements and lower-level floors—prime real estate for data centers.

Of course, major data centers in the New York metropolitan area had maintained backup generators, but many were located in basements, the first areas to flood after the storm hit. The centers that did manage to escape water damage faced another serious problem: a lack of fuel. The people who had designed disaster plans for their data centers never factored in that a power outage could last more than a few days. In short order, several centers all had the same message for their customers: Power down your servers and move your IT load someplace else—fast. Customers who were unable to comply lost data access, and in some instances their information was compromised or destroyed.

There are important IT lessons to be learned from the aftermath of Hurricane Sandy. First, when preparing a business continuity plan, never underestimate the potential for long-lasting turmoil. Second, your organization's IT systems should have failover capability spread across several widespread geographic locations. The recovery from data loss will be easier to weather if systems have been diversified. Otherwise, data recovery may prove impossible.

Acts of Terror: 9/11

In 1993, the World Trade Center (WTC) in New York City was the site of a significant terrorist attack when a truck bomb was detonated in an underground parking garage of the WTC's North Tower, killing several people and injuring more than a thousand in a deplorable act of terrorism.

In the aftermath of the bombing, which caused structural damage totaling about half a billion dollars, organizations located in the WTC and throughout New York City earnestly began reviewing and developing plans for disaster preparedness, business continuity, and data recovery. WTC-based enterprises also spent vast amounts of time and money on updating their resources in preparation for the potentially dangerous millennial date shift from 1999 to 2000 (also known as Y2K). Consequently, at the time 9/11 occurred, the World Trade Center had been arguably one of the best-prepared sites in the world for withstanding another attack or large-scale IT failure.

But the acts of violence perpetrated on 9/11, which resulted in the loss of nearly 3,000 lives and destroyed the WTC Towers, far exceeded anyone's expectations. The human tragedy, which was felt across the United States and around the world, left an indelible mark on our collective consciousness.

The destruction wrought on that day also revealed the inadequacy of IT preparedness plans. Despite all the preparation, and forethought that followed the 1993 bombing, the scale of the disaster proved far greater than organizations could have predicted. Careful planning generally mitigated data loss, particularly among larger companies, but IT equipment was obliterated. The cost of restoring IT to the WTC financial sector alone amounted to more than $5 billion.

Located near the WTC, the New York Stock Exchange (NYSE) was evacuated. Although its premises and much of its IT infrastructure escaped serious damage, it closed for several days after 9/11, largely because damaged phone-switching equipment in Lower Manhattan prevented communication for more than half of NYSE traders. The exchange resumed operations on Monday, September 17, and within a month the Dow, S&P, and NASDAQ indexes attained pre-9/11 price levels. Other financial organizations nearby did not fare as well. More than half of all small-to-mid-sized financial service enterprises permanently shut down.[6] For many of them, it was decimated IT infrastructure that played the critical role in their business failure.

Of the many IT lessons that must be learned from 9/11, the most salient takeaways for the industry are found in the shortcomings of the World Trade Center's disaster-response and continuity plans. For example, poor communication, or the lack of it, was commonplace and was only exacerbated by the general confusion that ensued following the attacks. Many firms in the area, including the New York Board of Trade, had no way of knowing which employees had survived the attack. They resorted to calling people individually during a time of disabled landlines and cell-phone service.

Other companies, such as Barclays Bank, had contingency plans for emergency relocation. Employees were to regroup at offices in New Jersey, but the plans were untested and fell short. The bridges and tunnels connecting New York and New Jersey were closed immediately after the attacks, and the temporary offices proved too small to accommodate the workers who did manage to arrive.

Contingency plans for electrical power outages relied heavily on the use of generators, few of which could keep pace with demand, their function being impeded or prevented entirely by the toxic dust that had blanketed Lower Manhattan. In many instances, the operators had not ordered enough fuel, and so generators could only work for a short time, which was insufficient given the extended power outage. (Many of these same problems would plague the city during Hurricane Sandy.)

The events of 9/11 will long echo in history. Among the legacies left behind was the impetus for organizations to revisit, revise, improve, and test disaster-response and enterprise continuity plans. Regardless, the threat of terroristic attacks persists, although now with an added layer of complexity: Unlike 9/11, future attacks worldwide could well originate from within the country being attacked. As Chapter 8 will examine, terrorist organizations like ISIS have radicalized and trained an unknown number of disaffected citizens, most of whom are recruited via social media. Consequently, both foreign and domestic terror must be viewed as a present and growing danger to the IT infrastructure of virtually every national institution.

"We are survival machines—robot vehicles blindly programmed to preserve the selfish molecules known as genes. This is a truth that still fills me with astonishment."

—Richard Dawkins, *The Selfish Gene*

Chapter 6

Wolves at the Door

Just a few years after the 9/11 attacks, the digital world began showing signs of sudden, profound change. Malware development, which had been nearly flat for about 25 years, suddenly doubled. By 2011, the rate at which new malware was being introduced had increased to about 60,000 unique new pieces per day. At the time of this writing, the rate-per-day number was close to 400,000—and it is still rising (Figure 1).[1] Even manufacturers of antivirus products have reservations about their ability to keep pace with this malware tidal wave, which coincides with several other major technological and cultural shifts. During this time:

- Digital information became part of the "commanding heights" of the world economy, critical to both national infrastructure and nearly all personal activities.
- High-speed Internet access became a global phenomenon by opening the Web to billions of new users, including millions of potential cybercriminals.
- Globalization and religious fundamentalism reshaped politics and polarized world communities.
- Transnational crime rates soared and the Web became a means to promote criminal agendas.

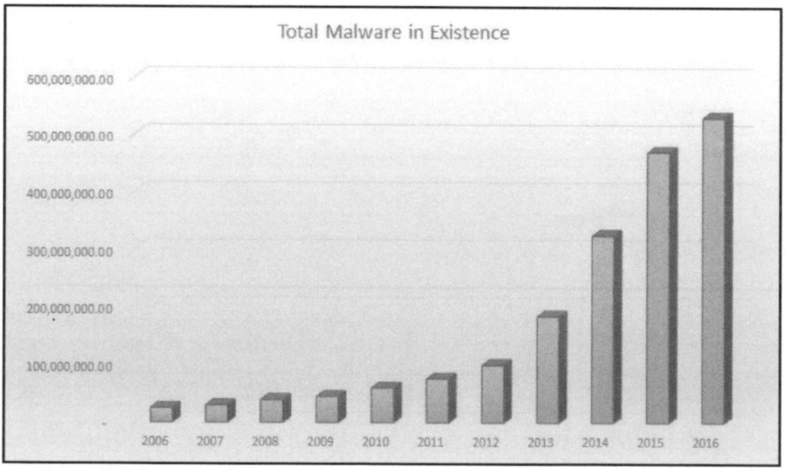

Fig. 1 Total pieces of malware in existence now tops 500 million.

Taken together, these events permanently transformed the digital world into a strange new place with an unknown geography and potential perils of incalculable scope and size. Society now generates information at incredible rates: Ninety percent of all the data that exists in the world today was created in just the past two years,[2] giving criminals and malcontents plenty of targets and opportunities to flex their muscles online and compromise these digital assets. And their methods are as varied as their motives. In the past, criminal elements looking to make money from breaching personally identifiable information stole copies of data that could then be sold on the "darknet" to those seeking to profit from identity fraud. "Spamming" once referred to the inappropriate use of e-mail to promote products or services, and the word "hacktivist" originally referred to a person or entity who used computers and computer networks to expose human rights violations or inappropriate corporate practices. These forms of digital invasion were serious violations, but they rarely caused harm or thwarted access to the actual data that they copied or exposed.

Unfortunately, as we shall see, these attacks have since evolved in more dangerous ways, becoming tools of digital extortion and posing serious threats to digital preservation. Every day brings new malware, crimes, and sophisticated schemes to rob, destroy, or prevent access to intellectual property. Understanding the nature of the threats, obstacles, and malicious attacks that are now possible in a world remade by the Digital Revolution is the first step to crafting successful countermeasures for digital preservation.

Ransomware

An executive at a mid-sized U.S. business enters her office at 10 a.m. to review some new Excel worksheets, but they cannot be found. In fact, she cannot access files of any type on the company network, and everyone else at the firm is having the same problem: The company's data has been maliciously encrypted by a hacker.

A ransom note fills every computer screen. To regain your data, the message states, you must deposit a specified amount of money into a bitcoin account or other untraceable digital wallet. Pay up or lose everything. Paying the ransom provides an encryption key to unlock the files. Without the key, the data will remain encrypted and useless. No matter what choice the company makes, however, it will probably need to replace all the affected hardware and all its storage media as a matter of security.

Although digital extortion is not new, the widespread use of ransomware is a relatively new phenomenon that dates back to around 2005. The first ransomware had its roots in one of the malware capitals of the world, Russia, and worked by compressing selected file types (such as "doc" or "exe" files) into zipped, password-protected data. Victims who paid the ransom would receive the password required for restoration. A short time later, Russian malefactors developed a ransomware variant that could infect a hard drive's master boot record so that the malware relaunched with each system reset.

The use of ransomware was mostly restricted to Russia until 2012, after which it began appearing in Europe and North America. Newer versions of ransomware, such as CryptoLocker, CryptoWall, and their relatives, are especially virulent since they propagate easily via e-mail attachments (typically sent through spam campaigns) and removable drives.

Other vectors used to spread the malware include exploit kits, a set of software tools that target security gaps found in vulnerable applications. Often delivered in the guise of legitimate updates or fixes, exploit kits are today responsible for an inordinately large share of malware. Applications considered most attack-prone to exploit kits include popular downloads like Adobe Acrobat Reader and Adobe Flash.[3] Malefactors use them to plant malware (such as the Crypto series) and gain control over PCs.

So-called "drive-by" ransomware is also on the rise and can involve nothing more than clicking on a website after being directed there by an e-mail or pop-up window. Unfortunately, there is generally little warning before a network suddenly succumbs to ransomware or some other malevolent presence.

Once present on a local host PC, ransomware establishes communication (a "handshake") with a remote server. The local malware scrambles data using 256-bit encryption (which even the U.S. National Security Agency (NSA) finds difficult or impossible to decode), while the remote server becomes the sole source of the decryption code. In addition to encrypting files, some forms of ransomware also delete backup data to prevent restoration. Because it sets keys in the Windows registry, most crypto-ransomware restarts every time an infected computer boots.

Part of ransomware's stealth is attributed to the anonymity of the bitcoin payment system, as well as to Tor software, which lets users engage in a full range of online activities without allowing identities or locations to be traced. This anonymity is paying off, literally. According to the U.S. Department of Justice, in 2014 ransomware earned its perpetrators about $27 million in just two months.[4] In partnership with the international community, the FBI made stopping this malware scheme a priority and managed to weaken CryptoLocker operations significantly that same year. Agents disabled malware servers and broke up the botnet (a network of hijacked computers infected with malware and controlled as a group without the owners' knowledge). The FBI also brought criminal charges against CryptoLocker mastermind and administrator, Evgeniy Mikhailovich Bogachev, a Russian hacker (who is discussed in Chapter 7). Ransomware attacks slumped for a while, but are now again on the rise, with CryptoLocker (and its CryptoWall variant) stronger than ever.[5] Some of the new entries into the ransomware market, Locky being one, no longer require user interaction, such as by clicking on a link. The malware can target weaknesses in server security and automatically start the encryption process. The security software company Trend Micro foresees unabated growth in ransomware, noting that this type of malware will likely continue to feature new functions as well as improved stealth capabilities.[6]

Because the use of crypto-ransomware is so lucrative, many established and aspiring cybercriminals want a piece of the action. Intel Security's McAfee reports the availability on the darknet of a free ransomware generator called Tox, stating that the malware functions "as advertised."[7] Just fill in a few data fields to send personalized ransomware to a chosen victim (Figure 2). Just one person—a competitor, enemy, or former employee—could cost an organization big money or put it out of business entirely. Tox's author benefited from giving away the free ransomware toolkit by collecting a 20-percent cut of the bitcoin ransom payoff.

At first glance, it may seem that the only response to a ransomware attack is to simply pay the ransom and move on. However, extortionists are hardly an honorable group, and so even a timely ransom payment provides no guarantee of regaining access to data. And even after making the payoff and receiving the key, information integrity might have already been compromised. Problems with data reliability and quality occur most often when PC users run an antivirus program on freshly decrypted data.[8]

Fig. 2 The Tox website makes it easy to create an executable virus file. It will even track ransomware installs and profits.

According to analysts and industry experts, in the coming years we can expect to see a proliferation of more sophisticated, lower-profile ransomware on Windows, Mac, and Android operating systems. For a criminal individual or organization, ransomware is an especially appealing crime, featuring low risk and high profits for minimal investment. As with other highly toxic malware, ransomware raises an important question: How well-prepared is your organization to protect and preserve its information?

In working with a single medium for tier-1 and tier-2 storage, even backups are easily compromised, and this is especially true when malware targets disk firmware and easily reinstalls or propagates. Even the author's own company experienced this issue when its IT systems were infected with ransomware. Although the malware associated with the attack did not propagate extensively, it was necessary to clear the infected systems, replace all the hard drives involved, and restore the information from a second medium that was known to be isolated (in this case, digital tape). No ransom was paid and no data was lost. This is a good example of how genetic diversity in storage can be a simple and effective method of assuring digital preservation.

Spam

Most of us consider spam a persistent, petty nuisance—an inescapable consequence of using e-mail. Assisted by special applications or our IT groups, we use filters, whitelists, traps, and other methods to minimize spam's infiltration of our inbox. Even so, spam continues. Why is it so prevalent? Does it pose serious threats to individual and enterprise systems? And who are the individuals and organizations promoting spam?

On one level, spam is a mass-marketing e-mail tool that specializes in promoting the sale of a product, often a variety of prescription drugs such as Viagra. It is difficult to imagine who could possibly be naïve enough to entrust their health to an anonymous online transaction that originated with spam. Nevertheless, many people do respond to junk e-mail. Noted journalist, security analyst, and author Brian Krebs acquired a list of more than one million people who had purchased prescription drugs through spam promotions. In interviews, he learned that buyers were attracted to the virtual pharmacy's confidentiality and low prices, among other features. In most instances, drug quality did not appear to be a concern. How do such dicey propositions succeed? The answer is simple: numbers. Considering that in 2013 nearly three-quarters of the global e-mail traffic sent every day was spam—roughly 85 billion pieces per day[9]—there are bound to be plenty of clicks through to websites.

Fig. 3 This graphic appears on a botnet tutorial site that provides tips on how to set up and install a variety of botnets.

To simultaneously deliver these billions of e-mails, spammers use Internet service providers (ISP) that specialize in the spam market and continue to operate illegally despite complaints from users, governments, and other organizations. Their geographic locations are difficult to pinpoint, although, in addition to the United States, they probably operate out of North Korea, Japan, China, and Russia, among other countries.[10] To augment the servers, spammers also do their best to infect PCs, phones, and other digital devices with malware, often converting devices into zombie botnet members that deliver still more spam and malware (Figure 3).

Infected spam messages, particularly those containing attachments or links to malicious URLs, are now among the largest vectors of malware in the world. In the workplace specifically, spam can make its way into operations in different ways. An employee might use a company network PC to unwittingly open a malicious spam-based URL. Similarly, someone could plug in a USB flash drive infected by spam malware for botnet conversion. In either case, the result would be the same as a direct spam attack on your company that can compromise your daily operations, customers, vendors, and brand identity.

Hopefully an enterprise's IT department has established fairly effective filters to block as much incoming spam as possible. However, as spam (and malware in general) becomes more sophisticated and difficult to detect, it will pose an increasing risk to both individuals and organizations. Even if filters do a passable job of eliminating spam, they are seldomly effective all of the time. As noted earlier, a spammer's success is based on the numbers game: Just one mishandled message, URL, or attachment can corrupt a system or entire network. While good policies cannot give back wasted time or resources, archived data can be better protected from corruption and theft with better data preservation workflows and increased diversity.

Hacktivism

Part political activist, part computer hacker, a hacktivist subversely uses computers and computer systems to disrupt the status quo and make headlines, generally with regard to a social or political cause. Hacker and publisher Julian Assange is a notable example, famous for his distribution of classified U.S. military information and diplomatic cables via WikiLeaks, the journalistic organization that he is credited with founding in 2006. Assange later expanded the scope of his leaks to include documents related to healthcare policy, trade deals, and other political topics. Revered in some circles and reviled in others, Assange reportedly lives under political asylum at the Embassy of Ecuador in London. *The New York Times* now describes WikiLeaks, once considered a quasi-political fringe organization, as a "watchdog group."[11]

Whether working alone or in a group of cyber vigilantes, a hacktivist acts as the target's judge, jury, and executioner. Perhaps an organization posts a Facebook comment that a hacktivist finds politically intolerable, or government policies or corporate management practices happen to fall on the wrong side of a hacktivist's beliefs. Maybe a hacktivist has confused you with someone else, and now you are on the hook. Be they right or wrong, it is easy for hacktivists to morally justify their actions, without the burden of accountability.

Anonymous

Like a head growing back on a mythical hydra, should one hacktivist be apprehended, another like-minded one will soon rise to fill his or her place. This is the major operating principle for the best known of all hacktivist groups, Anonymous, which typifies Carl Jung's famous saying, "The psychology of a large

crowd inevitably sinks to the level of a mob." Anonymous traces
its roots to the website 4chan, which was started in 2003 by a
15-year-old. It originally served as a message board used mainly
by male teenagers, most of whom bypassed the site's request
for a user name to opt for the default identity, "anonymous."
The main purpose of the site was to provide amusement and
entertainment, typically at the expense of others.

The forum was a hideout for "trolls," people who lurk in
online forums to humiliate other users, but it also attracted
more serious "doxxers," who hack into personal files or e-mail
accounts, then publish compromising information about the
victim online. Victim selection could be random or carefully
calculated.

One of the site's boards housed its most offensive content,
including images and comments directed against women, blacks,
Jews, gays, and others. By 2004, the board in question gained
recognition as a discrete unit called Anonymous. Over time, the
organization's culture evolved to include a more varied group
of individuals. A few years later Anonymous organized its first
"political" action: Project Chanology, a protest against the practices of the Church of Scientology. Anonymous's public relations
profile later improved in 2015, when it launched operations
against ISIS.

Not surprisingly, a significant number of "Anons" are hackers—about a fifth of them, according to a recent estimate—with
the rest being activists and techno nerds.[12] Today the group
appears ethnically diverse, but like the original 4chan group,
Anonymous members are predominantly male. When an Anon

appears in public rallies, he often wears a Guy Fawkes mask, popularized in the 2006 dystopian movie *V for Vendetta*. Many Anons fancy themselves as "digital Robin Hoods."

Structurally, Anonymous is more often described as a collective. Lacking hierarchy, it allows anyone to become an Anonymous member by simply proclaiming it so. The group has no clear leadership and, in theory, any member can issue a call to action. When the call occurs, it uses Internet Relay Chat or Twitter to coordinate thousands of users—sometimes internationally—to maximize the efficacy of attacks and demonstrations. The group counts on a large-scale tribal or "hive" response from its members and supporters.

It is rare for an Anonymous hacker to be arrested and used as an FBI informant. Hector "Sabu" Monsegur, however, is one of the few. Leader of the Anonymous splinter group known as LulzSec, Sabu played instrumental roles in cyber-attacks against Sony, Visa, MasterCard, and Nintendo, among other companies. His arrest then subsequent cooperation with the FBI led to the imprisonment of other Anonymous members, as well as members of related groups. After serving seven months' prison time and receiving a one-year probation, Monsegur reflected during an interview, "I find that a lot of companies…have no understanding of security whatsoever."[13]

The Birth of DDoS

In 2008, a video was leaked online that featured the actor Tom Cruise praising the Church of Scientology. The church responded by threatening legal action against anyone who shared its video content, online or otherwise. This enraged Anonymous members, many of whom marched publically to protest what they claimed was the church's unduly heavy hand.

During the same period, Anonymous was refining an existing software tool—Low Orbit Ion Cannon (LOIC)—for the purpose of disabling websites. Considered a legitimate software application, LOIC is used to send a series of small requests to a Web server, sometimes as a network stress test. However, LOIC is open-source software, written in C++, and in the public domain, which means that anyone can download and use it for any purpose, legitimate or otherwise. When used by one person, LOIC has little effect on a site's efficiency; however, when used in concert by a group of individuals (such as was planned by Anonymous), the site becomes overwhelmed with requests and fails to function. This act exemplifies a distributed denial-of-service (DDoS) attack. Anonymous used LOIC software to bring down the Church of Scientology website.

Fig. 4 The Anonymous logo.

Anonymous has gained the attention of top brass at the NSA and the Joint Chiefs of Staff for good reason. Could, and would, Anonymous or like groups disrupt the national power grid? Would an enemy of the United States provide Anonymous with more powerful malware capability? Janet Napolitano, the former secretary of the U.S. Department of Homeland Security, noted that in discussions of cyber-security threats, she often referred to Anonymous as her prime example. A former chief of cyber-security at the department observed that the federal government avoided comment on Anonymous in order to escape retribution. "Everyone is vulnerable," he said.[14]

In fact, vulnerability to an Anonymous attack extends to any individual, company, or organization. If, for whatever reason, Anonymous or one of its members decides that you are the enemy, you can anticipate being on the receiving end of a cyber-attack characterized by malice, humiliation, innuendo, and lies.

Recognizing, therefore, that today's DDoS attacks are one of the main, and most effective, weapons in the contemporary hacker's arsenal, what is the best defense against such an assault? Keep more Web servers online. In other words, the more power behind a website, the less likely it is to suffer from DDoS. Few organizations, however, can afford the cost of additional, high-performance servers dedicated solely to averting DDoS attacks.

Worse still, while most of the activities of a group like Anonymous have been based on DDoS or releasing hacked information, how long until Anonymous obtains and uses cyber weapons that are far more dangerous, or even deadly? Might one of the Anons decide, for example, that our carbon footprint is too large, and then proceed—with self-righteous fervor—to knock out our air-traffic control systems or power grid? When it comes to hackers in general, and Anonymous in particular, virtually everyone, and everything, is open to attack.

It is very important to recognize that these "lone wolf" attackers have evolved, and will continue to evolve, in their ability to interrupt businesses, services, and even government operations. It would be naïve of us to think that the threat they pose has leveled off. Anonymous is just one example of how individuals, grouped together in a joint effort, can significantly threaten the vehicles of information, as well as the information itself, that is used to run the modern world. As efforts continue to keep out the invaders, organizations must assign equal weight to reinforcing their capacity to rebuild if preventive efforts do fail.

The next chapter will examine how dangerously these stakes rise when cyber-attacks are organized by nation-states rather than by loosely organized social media groups.

"We often give our enemies the means for our
own destruction."

—Aesop (c. 600 BCE)

Chapter 7

From Cold War to Cyber War

Many positive developments of modern globalization might have
never occurred without the advantages brought about by the Digital
Revolution. Unfortunately, not all aspects of our worldwide digital connectivity serve us equally well—for as the political world
changes, so too does the cyber world.

Genetic diversity in the data center does little to protect against
long-practiced forms of political intrigue, such as espionage or the
theft of trade secrets, but it is often the only defense against the
outright destruction of data. Unlike the cyber-attacks described in
Chapter 6, a new form of subterfuge is being pioneered, not by anonymous hackers and criminals, but by hostile foreign governments.

We can begin, aptly, with the fall of the Soviet Union, which occurred in 1991, the same year that the World Wide Web made its public debut. America's traditional Cold War enemies—notably Russia, China, and North Korea—emerged from the contest with the seeds of future cybercrime already planted within them. During the Cold War, governmental oppression in the Eastern Bloc deprived many people of basic needs and simple luxuries. A black-market economy was the natural consequence, and organized crime became not only rampant but widely accepted as a necessary evil. In the chaotic aftermath of the Cold War, crime organizations grew even stronger and more influential, with extortion, murder, and human trafficking becoming facts of everyday life. Pervasive corruption blurred the lines between legitimate government and organized crime, and the rise of the Internet afforded new and powerful ways to pursue nefarious objectives. As a 2013 report from the Council on Foreign Relations notes:

> Over the past two decades, as the world economy has globalized, so has its illicit counterpart. The global impact of transnational crime has risen to unprecedented levels. Criminal groups have appropriated new technologies, adapted horizontal network structures that are difficult to trace and stop, and diversified their activities. The result has been an unparalleled scale of international crime.[1]

Russia: The Syndicate

Following the dissolution of the Soviet Union, its most powerful criminal syndicates gave birth to as many as 2,600 discrete gangs, 300 of which were considered "large syndicates."[2] Even worse was the interference of these new players in governmental affairs: In some places it was impossible to tell where the state ended and the mafia began. The effects of corruption could be seen even at the lowest levels of government. On average, half the income of a typical government worker in Russia came from bribes.[3]

The Russian syndicate kept pace with the development of new Internet technologies and soon began using the Web to perpetrate its crimes. For them, the online world offered many new, and arguably easier, ways to make money. Like Willie Sutton, the prolific American bank robber, they knew of no better place to find cash than from the world's largest banks.

Fig. 1 Evgeniy Mikhailovich Bogachev, ringleader of the Gameover Zeus cybercrime ring.

The FBI maintains a list of its 10 most-wanted cybercriminals, and at the top of the 2015 list is Evgeniy Mikhailovich Bogachev (Figure 1).[4] The U.S. State Department offers a reward of up to $3 million for information leading to the arrest or conviction of the man who created Zeus, a Trojan horse malware that has been used to steal hundreds of millions of dollars from United States and European banks. Although a fugitive, Bogachev is not living a life literally running from the law. Instead, he spends his time in a comfortable Black Sea resort home, basking in the admiration of his neighbors. As one of them told a reporter for *The Telegraph,* "What a talented guy. Sitting at his computer at home, he broke into our enemies' camp, but did not harm his fellow Russians."[5] The newspaper continues:

> ...such comments show how the anti-Americanism that has lain dormant in Russia since the end of the Cold War has re-erupted since the confrontation with the West over Ukraine. As lone agents exposing holes in America's cyber-defences, Russian cyberhackers are seen as combining the cunning of a KGB spy with the brains of a Soviet-era scientist.[6]

When asked about the apprehension of international cyber-criminals, Richard Clarke, former presidential security adviser to George W. Bush, summed up the situation in a single sentence: "The FBI has tried to get cooperation, the State Department has asked for help and nothing happens, so law enforcement options under the current circumstances are pretty negligible."[7]

The $1 billion job

Grand-scale theft is one of the Russian syndicate's specialties, and its operations are not limited to any specific country. In 2015 the press reported on one of the largest heists of all time. Russian hackers had stolen $1 billion from 100 banks in 30 countries.[8] They used ATMs to dispense cash (without any physical contact with the machines, instead sending mules to collect the money) and also transferred funds into fictitious accounts, limiting their take to about $10 million per bank. This hacking scheme of astounding proportions is believed to have gone undetected for as long as two years and, as of this writing, the perpetrators remain at large.

At least one U.S. bank lost millions in the Russian theft, although its management denies any losses despite contrary reports by intelligence and law-enforcement officials. As with its American mob counterparts, the Russian syndicate benefits from its victims' fear of acknowledging the crimes committed against them. In fact, most cybercrimes go unreported or are outrightly denied. To protect their interests, the victimized banks try to avoid publicly addressing several key questions: What happened to the bank's auditing systems? How did they overlook the existence of fictitious accounts or the millions of dollars that were transferred to them? Why did it take so long to discover the data breach?

Around the same time as the $1 billion theft, syndicate operatives had struck additional times, including stealing $45 million from ATMs, $50 million from the Internal Revenue Service, and 160 million credit card numbers, as well as hacking into the White House, Wall Street, NATO, and the U.K. government.[9] Referring to the Russian syndicate, Karim Hijazi, former CEO of the security firm Unveillance, observed, "The Russian Mafia are the most prolific cybercriminals in the world."[10]

Not only prolific, but perhaps unstoppable, as the cyber juggernaut continues, as seen with other cybercrimes that include commandeering U.S. military drones[11] and demonstrating the capability to sabotage U.S. power grids.[12]

China: Partner, Competitor, or Criminal?

Russia's nearest rival in the scope and power of its criminal activities is its old Cold War ally, China. In 2014 James Comey, director of the FBI, was of the opinion that Chinese hackers were not especially skilled, comparing them to drunk burglars, "…kicking in the front door, knocking over the vase, while they're walking out with your television set." Mostly, he said, "they're just prolific…."[13] The director could not have been more mistaken for, even as he spoke, China was in the midst of conducting a huge hack—possibly the largest one ever perpetrated against the U.S. government—specifically, against the Office of Personnel Management (OPM).

The breach, discovered by OPM in April 2015, was brought to the public's attention in June, with President Barack Obama announcing the discovery on a Thursday. While the next day's news was packed with hack-related headlines, by week's end the subject had largely disappeared from the public view. Over the next several weeks, however, news concerning the attack grew increasingly grim. Believed to have begun in March 2014, the breach was substantially larger and more far-reaching than originally announced, affecting more than 16 million people. Detailed personnel files of various types of government employees and contractors, both current and former, were hacked into, as were background files of U.S. military and intelligence agency staff.

OPM conducts nearly all federal background checks, including those of the Defense Department (DoD) and 100 other agencies, and these deep checks go back to 1985.[14] Such a store of highly sensitive data could help the Chinese test passwords for other government sites, including those holding information about U.S. weapons systems. The information about federal employee finances, compromising personal details, and foreign contacts, recorded in the stolen background check reports could also be used to blackmail U.S. agents. Sensitive FBI personnel information was also hacked, although an FBI source said he did not know the extent of the breach. He did note that OPM "outsourced some of their software to a Chinese company Unfortunately, I do not think anyone's going to be fired like they should be."[15]

In short order, a branch of Anonymous published the FBI e-mail addresses and passwords for dozens of agents, as well as the geographic coordinates of the FBI director's home. We do not yet know if the hacked information will compromise members of the CIA, however *The Washington Post* noted that it remains a possibility.[16]

The information stolen from the FBI and OPM will continue to affect the national security community of the United States for decades to come, although the full ramifications of the breach are not as yet known. *The Wall Street Journal* observed that "the staggering haul of records could amount to one of the biggest feats of espionage in decades," and asked, "When does a hack become an act of war?"[17]

Other questions arise as to why the breach was successful. Despite a long history of cyber-attacks against U.S. government agencies, OPM had no internal, security-certified IT staff until

2013.[18] What caused the delay? And why did OPM outsource its software development to China—a nation notorious for intellectual property theft, piracy, cybercrime, counterfeiting, and espionage against the United States? We may never hear satisfactory responses to these inquiries. Regardless, an overriding query persists: How do Chinese hackers manage to operate so successfully and covertly?

Fig.2 This FBI wanted poster of alleged Chinese hackers represents the first time that the agency named specific state actors in connection with hacking.

The answer lies in the high-caliber intellect and talent of the hackers themselves, who typically misdirect the efforts of forensic researchers by using false cyber evidence as part of their standard mode of operation. One of their favorite tricks is to permit a forensic expert to "discover" the source of a data breach when, in reality, the code found has been deliberately planted. In the meantime, hackers usually keep their most effective and dangerous malware out of the sight of even the most meticulous investigator for long periods of time. Once Chinese hackers have compromised a system, they maintain a presence there for one year on average. The longest recorded stay was just under five years.[19]

Other notable Chinese espionage-related hacks include the theft from the Pentagon and Martin Marietta of F-35 fighter-jet blueprints specifying the plane's radar, engine schematics, and other design components. (Since the theft, China's military has built two strikingly similar aircraft, the Shenyang J-31 and the Chengdu J-20 stealth fighters). According to DoD documents published by WikiLeaks, hackers working within the Chinese People's Liberation Army are also to blame for stealing information related to U.S. space-based lasers, missile systems, submarines, the B-2 Spirit stealth bomber, and the F-22 Raptor stealth fighter. DoD estimates the amount of stolen data to be in excess of 50 terabytes.[20]

Because nearly all federal agencies, including OPM and DoD, rely on the work of civilian contractors, virtually every governmental data breach has had one or more breach counterparts in the private sector. In other words, the Chinese hack U.S. businesses with the same impunity with which they attack the U.S. government. Mike McConnell, a former NSA director, stated, "The Chinese have penetrated every major corporation of any consequence in the United States and taken information. We have never, ever not found Chinese malware."[21]

Diving deep into cyber-attacks coming out of Russia and China teaches us an important lesson: No entity is safe from cyber intrusion. Furthermore, no asset is safe—be it money, infrastructure, or data. How can the average U.S. organization maintain a robust level of security when major governmental departments and corporations with significantly greater security resources at their disposal are experiencing major breaches? More important, what if the end game for most of the cyber-attacks launched by hostile governments—theft—turns to destruction? Unfortunately, it is no longer a "what if" conversation.

North Korea: Bureau 121

Russia and China are considered superpowers, but when it comes to cyber-attacks, any nation can pose a lethal threat. Since the early 1950s, North Korea has been one of the most destitute, isolated countries in East Asia. For more than 40 years, it survived through the support of its communist allies, China and the Soviet Union. With the end of the Cold War in 1991, however, shipments of oil, rice, and money to North Korea ended and famine swept across the country. Today the vast majority of North Koreans live in poverty, with little to eat and practically no way to escape. The country's current leader, Kim Jong-un, has received much attention in the international press for being an eccentric, unpredictable dictator and a militant enemy of the United States and its Western allies.

Despite its circumstances of poverty and unpredictable leadership, North Korea is among the heavy hitters of cybercrime. Its military runs the Reconnaissance General Bureau, an agency focused on espionage and cyber-attacks. Within the agency, Bureau 121 is the military's most exclusive and powerful cybercrime unit, and its "hackers are among the most-talented, and rewarded, people in North Korea, handpicked and trained from as young as 17."[22] One of the bureau's outposts is purportedly located just over the border in China, in the basement of a restaurant.

One computer espionage expert and former member of the North Korean military has observed that "for [the military], the strongest weapon is cyber. In North Korea, it is called the Secret War."[23] This is a war being waged far beyond the scope of online crime. Prior to his defection, Kim Heung-Kwang, a computer-science professor for 20 years at a large North Korean college, taught many of the students who now belong to Bureau 121. Kim has told the BBC, "North Korean hackers are capable of attacks that could destroy critical infrastructure and even kill people."[24] He estimates the size of the military cyber-attack unit at around 6,000 people and believes the military allots up to 20 percent of its budget to online operations. According to Kim, North Korea wages its cyber-attacks via difficult-to-trace China based IP addresses.[25]

For decades, poverty and ineptitude had blunted North Korea's plans to damage U.S. and Western interests, however this has begun to change. In a preemptive move in 2010, the NSA began investigating selected Chinese networks used by North Korea, planting malware to trace Bureau 121 activities.[26] Yet only a few years later, North Korean operatives managed to successfully launch the most damaging attack ever waged against a major international corporation.

The Sony attack

It was as early as April 2014, when reports of suspicious cyber activity first began surfacing at Sony Corporation. Later that year, and a few weeks before a massive attack on Sony Pictures Entertainment, an e-mail from a group calling itself the Guardians of Peace was sent to its top executives. The message warned that, unless the company delivered a specified sum of money, "Sony Pictures will be bombarded as a whole."[27] It still remains unclear if the e-mail reached its destination or, if it did, how the executives responded.

Initial reports on the cyber-attack that unfolded against Sony Pictures in November 2014 downplayed the hack's power and scope; the company referred to the situation as merely an "IT matter." However, Sony would soon realize the full magnitude of the attack, and the public would learn more about the ways in which the studio had been compromised and embarrassed by leaks of internal correspondence and e-mails. The news gradually revealed the true extent of Sony's damages, including the hacker's claim that they possessed more than 100 terabytes of Sony data consisting of personnel records, executive salaries, social-security numbers, scripts, entire films awaiting release, usernames and passwords, phone numbers, and a seemingly endless list of personal information about the firm's employees.

Consequently, for weeks after the attack, Sony deliberately pushed its business operations back in time about 30 years.

Fearing additional attacks or digital violations, Sony shut down all its internal e-mail systems, online services, and computer hardware and software operations. Smartphones were no longer allowed—landlines were considered far more secure. Invoices were written out by hand. When they needed to distribute a memo, employees were told to try the fax machine or go to the post office.

This is precisely the type of scenario that can play out in any organization victimized by a hack. Until all investigations, forensics, and data integrity checks are completed, in-house IT is unavailable and useless. How well would your business function today if it had to revert to snail mail and fax machines? What would happen to operations, profits, and productivity? What if the customers or vendors that you rely on were also attacked? Would your enterprise even survive? These and other issues must be addressed proactively and comprehensively by any individual or organization that maintains a presence in an online world fraught with digital peril.

If there was any motivation for the Sony hack, it appeared to stem at least in part from Sony's then-forthcoming feature film, *The Interview*, a satire about a U.S. journalist who befriends, with the intent to assassinate, North Korea's supreme leader. The film, and Sony's bungling of its release, still haunts the company today.

Unsurprisingly, the North Korean government steadfastly denied any knowledge about the attacks against Sony, however U.S. agencies and independent cyber-security companies do not take their claims seriously. The Destover malware used in the hack included Korean language code, and Symantec noted a connection between Destover and other malware intended to attack South Korean targets. Software company Kaspersky Lab and Symantec both observed a relationship between Destover and Shamoon, the malware used in the 2012 attack against Saudi Aramco (a major Saudi Arabian oil and natural gas company). In what was likely the final nail in the culpability coffin, the NSA was able to reference the spyware that it had planted a few years earlier in the North Korean cybercrime system.

The Sony attack still rates among one of the largest digital assaults in history. IDC estimates that it cost Sony over $250 million.[28] CNN called the attack "nightmarish" and said that it "blows a massive crater in the Sony brand."[29] From a cyber-security perspective, however, the hack's most remarkable feature was the calculated destruction of data. The assault against Sony was executed not just to hack, but to eradicate information held by a large corporate entity. As noted in *The New York Times*, "Mountains of documents had been stolen, internal data centers had been wiped clean, and 75 percent of the servers had been destroyed."[30]

Journalists, analysts, and security experts have tried to make sense of this new, destructive approach to hacking. Tenable Security's chief executive, Ron Gula, voiced a consensus opinion that "hackers are moving from stealing data to destroying it" and that these attackers "will move from exfiltration to pure destruction of data."[31] Michael Chertoff, co-founder of the Chertoff Group and former secretary of the U.S. Department of Homeland Security, reached a similar conclusion. "Either for political or economic reasons, at some point sophisticated actors are going to be more willing to use destructive malware."[32]

Due to the sensitive nature of cyber-attacks, the full extent of Sony's data loss and the associated costs of that loss will likely never be revealed; the numbers quoted in this writing are estimates. There are many challenges to "putting things back to normal" after a cyber-attack, but when the only surviving copy of valuable information is lost, data restoration can be the one insurmountable feat. Often, data simply cannot be reproduced, no matter how much money is spent on recovery.

The Sony hack is just one more cautionary tale to add to the list of alarming trends in the natural and human-engineered threats posed to the digital universe. As previous chapters have described, severe, damaging storms are occurring more frequently, hackers are becoming more sophisticated and dangerous, and nation-states, once concerned only with intelligence gathering against other political bodies, are now also working to debilitate companies and private organizations. But as Chapter 8 will reveal, there are even greater threats looming on the horizon. A new brand of attack—one focused not only on society's genome itself, but also on the infrastructures that support and protect both it and the world at large—is a reality that we must confront.

"Should a nuclear event eradicate most of life on earth, but not all life, some rat or bacteria will emerge out of nowhere, perhaps the bottom of the oceans, and the story will start again, without us, and without the members of the Office of Management and Budget, of course."

—Nassim Nicholas Taleb, *Antifragile: Things That Gain from Disorder*

Chapter 8

The Unthinkable

Although disturbing to imagine, a sophisticated attack against national cyber systems could instantly disable any industrialized country. Power grids could fail, and not for just a few minutes, but for days—or longer. Financial markets and banks could shut down indefinitely, telecommunications, including cell-phone service, could be silenced, and even military systems could be compromised.

Such a scenario falls beyond the scope of natural disasters and human error and enters the world of the unthinkable, where the collapse of critical infrastructures leaves the fate of civilization hanging in the balance. There would be no shortage of suspects in such an apocalyptic tale, with Russia, China, North Korea, and the Islamic State group, also known as ISIS, all potentially profiting from the destruction of the infrastructure and institutions of the Western world. Threats to digital preservation lie closer to home as well. Even the NSA operates its own secret force of exceptional power and cyber virtuosity. As unthinkable as these threats might be, it would be unwise to ignore the potential of a cataclysmic attack. Once infrastructure is rebuilt or repaired, the continuance of government, society, and life as we know it will depend on restoring as much of the previous information as possible.

Weaponized Electromagnetic Interference

Electromagnetic interference (EMI) is popularly (and often incorrectly) referred to as an EMP, or an electromagnetic pulse. EMI describes the interruption of an electronic device that can occur when the device is in the vicinity of an electromagnetic field. EMI can arise from naturally occurring sources, such as lightning or solar storms, but it can also be man-made. Whatever its source, EMI has a documented history of disabling electrical components and power systems, as well as "confusing" electronics into atypical, lethal behavior (as we will later see).

Apart from the vast array of malware discussed in earlier chapters, weaponized EMI probably poses the gravest peril for digital information and long-term digital preservation. Often inexpensive, portable, and readily available, EMI weapons have been compared to nuclear armaments in their capacity to inflict destruction and chaos. Yet the private sector and even most governments have done little to prepare for EMI assaults. When deployed, EMI weapons can wipe out every piece of electrical and electronic equipment for miles around, including virtually all the critical infrastructure within its blast radius, as well as hard drives, vehicle-ignition systems, and more. A smaller, more focused EMI attack could target a single business or even just one individual.

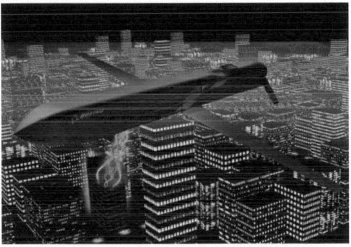

Fig. 1 The Counter-Electronics High Power Microwave Advanced Missile Project—or CHAMP—is a militaristic EMI device. During a 2012 test flight, it discharged a burst of high-power microwaves that brought down the testing compound's entire spectrum of electronic systems.[1]

Weaponized EMI has deep roots that go back to the early 1950s, when the British military began testing its nuclear weapons. Royal Air Force pilots noticed that following a nuclear blast many of their onboard electrical instruments would immediately fail. They recognized the cause as an electromagnetic anomaly, which they called a "radioflash," that could destroy or damage a variety of electronic devices if left unprotected by heavily shielded cables and Faraday cages (enclosures built of grounded metal screening).

About a decade later, the U.S. government executed a truly bizarre and dangerous plan to detonate a hydrogen bomb—a weapon 100 times stronger than the one used at Hiroshima in 1945—high above the earth's atmosphere. Among other things, officials wanted to determine if the radiation released by the bomb could alter the Van Allen radiation belts—with the intention of expediting an American nuclear attack against Moscow. The Van Allen belts are doughnut-shaped zones of highly energetic charged particles that encircle the earth and are held together by the planet's magnetic field, with the inner belt extending from about 600 miles to about 3,700 miles above the planet's surface.

Code-named Starfish Prime, the 1962 test was the first successful test in a series of high-altitude nuclear tests known as Operation Fishbowl. It involved detonating a 1.44-megaton bomb 250 miles above the mid-Pacific Ocean. The resulting electromagnetic disturbance—far greater than anything anticipated by U.S. authorities—knocked out hundreds of streetlights and shut down phone communications in the Hawaiian Islands, nearly 900 miles away.[2] The increased radiation left behind by the detonation apparently also disabled several satellites, including Ariel 1, the U.K.'s first satellite, and Telstar 1, the world's first commercial relay communication satellite.

Most of the government equipment intended to measure Starfish Prime's effects were rendered useless as well. Fortunately, there was no lasting impact to the Van Allen radiation belts, but the United States learned an important lesson: Electromagnetic devices can serve as weapons with a profoundly destructive potential.

Fig. 2 The fire aboard the *Forrestal* killed 134 men and injured another 161, with damage to the ship exceeding $72 million (about $511 million in today's dollars).

Another example of EMI's shockingly destructive powers occurred accidentally in July 1967 aboard the USS *Forrestal* supercarrier as it was preparing for combat missions in Vietnam. Because of a tiny, undetected mechanical failure, a jet on the flight deck began randomly firing its munitions. (A pilot on the flight deck at the time was U.S. Senator John McCain, who was then a lieutenant commander.) The ensuing explosions and fires killed 134 crewmen and injured another 161, as well as severely damaged the ship. Navy investigations revealed the disaster's cause: a degraded cable-shield termination on the jet.[3] A single faulty cable termination, combined with EMI from the *Forrestal*'s radar, had led to one the deadliest incidents of America's post–WWII naval history.

Today terrorists and criminals can use intentional electro-magnetic interference (IEMI) as a weapon to disrupt, damage, or destroy a wide range of electrical and electronics systems.[4] In its 2010 report to U.S. Department of Energy's Oak Ridge National Laboratory, scientists and engineers from the Metatech Corporation reached several disturbing conclusions regarding IEMI:[5]

- Electromagnetic fields can penetrate virtually any physical boundary.
- EMI-based criminal activities can be executed covertly and anonymously.
- Likely targets of intentional EMI include critical infrastructure and societal needs, such as transportation, communications, security systems, and medicine.
- Severe disruptions of national health and economic activities could ensue.

A recent analysis in *The Wall Street Journal* echoed these findings, noting that an EMI attack would cause "staggering devastation."[6] Greatly magnifying these concern is the fact that nearly anyone—including terrorists and criminals—can build small-scale, although still highly destructive, IEMI devices using instructions and materials available online. Depending on the weapon's size and capabilities, the cost can range from about $200 to $2,500 (Figure 3).

The effectiveness of these EMI weapons is frightening. For instance, a small mobile EMI device—placed in the bed of a pickup truck—can destroy or impair virtually all electronics within a 600-foot radius. It can also simultaneously "corrupt and disrupt the data of commerce over two miles away."[7] The attacker could then drive off undetected.

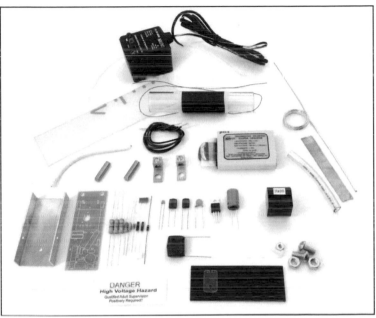

Fig. 3 This $200 kit is for a handheld, low-power EMP gun advertised to be able to deprogram and disrupt microprocessor circuitry.

The power and accuracy of EMI weapons can also vary. One weapon could destroy entire power grids, while another could fry all the electronics within a targeted city. Others might only disable the smartphone on your desk. However, a nuclear-based IEMI weapon has the capacity to inflict large-scale damage and loss of life. When detonated a few hundred miles above the earth, a nuclear bomb releases a wave of gamma rays into the upper atmosphere. Once the electromagnetic pulse reaches the earth's surface, it would destroy all electrical and electronic components in its path, from household appliances and micro-processors to the grids that control power and communication.

So who has this capability and would they leverage it? North Korea may already possess the nuclear weapons technology required to initiate such an attack, and other countries could gain such a capability. Even if they do not obtain the technology to launch global strikes, a devastating EMI attack could still be executed from a smaller distance. For example, a container ship in the Gulf of Mexico could serve as the launching platform for a nuclear EMI attack against the United States that would quickly disable American infrastructure and cause mass casualties. As defense analysts R. James Woolsey and Peter Vincent Pry observed in *The Wall Street Journal*, "A nuclear device detonated above the U.S. could kill millions, and we've done almost nothing to prepare."[8]

Nonnuclear electromagnetic weapons also exist and involve using technologies such as capacitor banks and microwave generators. Although the radius of their detonations cannot compare with those of nuclear-based IEMI weapons, they can wreak the same type of destruction, albeit on a smaller scale.

From an IT perspective, it should be apparent by now that EMI can disable or destroy all of an organization's computers, servers, and printers, as well as the old fax machine down the hall and the coffeemaker next to it. The central question is whether all your information—your organization's genome—is recoverable, and at what cost and with how much time. The answer varies depending on how and where the information is stored, as well as the types of media on which it is stored.

For example, purpose-built data centers shield against EMI through a combination of protective measures that might include

EMI-resistant building architecture,[9] Faraday-style enclosures around sensitive equipment, and a combination of storage media, such as tape or optical media, to mitigate hard-drive failures. Unfortunately, despite the clear threat posed by EMI and the proven methods to protect against it, most digital information in the United States is vulnerable to EMI attack, a vulnerability that stems from a lack of diversity. Keeping all data online, using just one type of media, and having all copies of data located within a narrow geographic range makes it much more likely for a single event to corrupt or destroy a major portion of an organization's data.

At the very least, organizations have the power to preserve their essential information on multiple media types and thus gain a head start on rebuilding. Enterprises can easily fortify their data availability by such a move, yet today the trend is to move away from diversified media and toward disk-only or cloud-only based storage. Why aren't organizations being more proactive? The answer is that hard drives and cloud storage are seemingly inexpensive and secure. They are also perceived as being different storage media, despite the fact that cloud storage usually comprises hard drives, making its primary function not diversity in media but diversity in geography. The fact is, however, that this geographic distance is rarely substantial.

Different storage media respond differently to EMI, and these differences are detailed in the next chapter, which will also explain how to add to or increase the diversity of your organization's genome.

ISIS: Cyber Evangelists of Destruction

Perhaps one of the most confounding and least predictable potential users of IEMI is the religious fundamentalist and extremist group ISIS (known also as the Islamic State group or ISIL or Daesh). A splinter group of al-Qaeda in Iraq, ISIS came into being for a variety of reasons, including the chaos in Iraq and a civil war in Syria. It is, however, one of the fastest-growing, best-funded military forces in the Middle East, known for its brutal killings of "enemies," including other Muslims, Christians, Jews, Westerners, journalists, or anyone else who has the misfortune of being caught in their crosshairs. It has also claimed responsibility for terrorist attacks in Europe and other regions. The group's main goals are to spread their violent brand of Islam around the world and eradicate everyone—and everything—not in accord with their beliefs.

ISIS military forces have performed well against nearly all opposition, and the U.S. response has been somewhat hesitant and ill-defined. The CIA's estimates of ISIS's military strength seem similarly conflicting, ranging from just a few hundred soldiers several years ago to more than 30,000 today. In contrast, a Kurdish official has stated that the number of ISIS fighters is at least 200,000, which could explain how the group maintains so much manpower over so many battlegrounds.[10] Whatever the case, in the midst of war, it seems impossible to determine an accurate answer.

At the time of this writing, ISIS commanded about one-third of both Syria and Iraq, an area about the size of Great Britain. In 2014, ISIS declared itself a caliphate, meaning that it was a divinely sanctioned Muslim government led by a political and religious descendant of Muhammad. The government's leader, or caliph, is ISIS founder and leader, Abu Bakr al-Baghdadi. Educated, wealthy, and politically well-connected, al-Baghdadi is an indiscriminate killer.

Part of the confusion surrounding the size and appeal of ISIS stems from the fact that new conscripts from around the world are constantly joining and strengthening its ranks. The group has established footholds in other areas, including Libya, and other groups have affiliated themselves with ISIS.

Few other political entities use the Web as effectively as does ISIS, which especially excels at recruiting new soldiers via Twitter and other social media outlets. Their recruitment campaigns have been successful in the United States and Western Europe, especially with teenagers and young adults. ISIS will often entice potential recruits to come fight in Syria and Iraq. Sometimes the organization provides training to young people in order to form an ISIS presence back in their home countries. In either case, ISIS receives responses, and many Americans and Europeans—nearly 20 percent of whom are women—have chosen to support the group. From 2014 to 2015, the number of foreign fighters joining ISIS increased by 80 percent.[11]

Masterful in its use of social media for propaganda and recruiting, ISIS has so far done relatively little in the realm of cybercrime. To date, most ISIS cybercrimes can be rated as low-level acts: hacking social media accounts, vandalizing websites, and mounting denial-of-service attacks.

ISIS wages physical war on everyone who fails to support its caliphate. But what of cyber war? For all the terror and fear it spreads, why are its efforts so weak in this area? A military tactician would instead advise abundant caution: When a strong, capable enemy does far less than you expect, it is time to prepare for the worst. NSA officials and other security experts agree that we can anticipate far more intensive action from ISIS on the cyber front. Specifically, it is believed that ISIS will eventually gain access to large-scale malware and other cyber weapons. According to the cyber-security firm, FireEye, "The Islamist militants who have seized almost a third of Iraq and Syria pose the next great cyber threat as terrorist organizations hoard cyber weaponry from underground markets."[12]

For the right price, a user can buy powerful, disabling cyber tools from online sources such as eBay or the darknet, which facilitates the black market and anonymous transactions. The cost may range from several thousand to tens of thousands of dollars, and the user does not need high levels of expertise to operate these tools. FireEye also anticipates that Islamist militants will "aim for a target as big and sensationalized as possible."[13]

Even if ISIS lacks the expertise to execute a significant cyber-attack, it can easily bring in outside talent—such as the Russian syndicate—and fund its campaigns through the sale of oil.

TAO and the Stuxnet Experience

Much of the responsibility for computer surveillance conducted since 9/11 has fallen to the NSA, known for its talents in espionage and cyber warfare. America's status as a premiere international cyber warrior is due in no small measure to this agency, and in particular to the elite hackers who work in the Office of Tailored Access Operations (TAO), the cyber-warfare intelligence-gathering unit. These NSA specialists develop and plant malware on behalf of U.S. security interests. *Der Spiegel* has referred to this top operative group as being "something like a squad of plumbers that can be called in when normal access to a target is blocked."[14]

In 2008, when the United States decided to obstruct the progress of nuclear programs in Iran, the NSA and TAO developed Stuxnet, a computer worm created to damage industrial control systems that regulate automated machinery, such as assembly lines and centrifuges. Typically introduced into a PC via an infected USB flash drive or optical media, Stuxnet was a huge success, ultimately destroying nearly 20 percent of Iran's nuclear centrifuges. Without a shot having to be fired, an enemy state was subdued, at least temporarily, making Stuxnet more than just malware. It was a foreign policy tool that fulfilled American political objectives while circumventing the need for military intervention.

Skeptics, on the other hand, viewed Stuxnet and the NSA from a different, darker perspective. The terrifying beauty of the Stuxnet worm is that it did nothing to alter normal PC behavior. It was able to remain undetected, even as it played havoc with Iran's nuclear industrial control systems. This represents an underlying principle of NSA software, termed "command and control," or C&C. With Stuxnet's C&C in place, the NSA could gain full, remote access and control of both the computers and the machinery regulated by them.

What, then, would prevent the NSA from using Stuxnet against unwarranted targets, such as U.S. allies or American citizens? How would the NSA prevent Stuxnet technology from falling into the hands of criminals and rogue nations? For that matter, why should we blindly trust one of the world's most powerful clandestine organizations? There are no satisfactory answers here. The NSA remains cloaked in silence, secrecy, and power, and its masterpiece, Stuxnet, is perhaps one of the most ingenious and effective pieces of malware ever developed.

The Equation Group

In early 2015, analysts at Kaspersky Lab announced that they had discovered hard drives that had had their firmware reprogrammed with malware. In some cases, the malware had remained undiscovered for more than a decade. (Located on the drive's circuit board and platters, firmware essentially contains the hard drive's operating system.)

The code that Kaspersky Lab found bore at least a few signatures of the NSA, including the capability to command and control computers remotely. Kaspersky stated that the malware's creators belonged to what it called the Equation Group, a name based on the code's sophisticated mathematics. Although it has been difficult to prove, it is commonly accepted that the malware's author was, as Kaspersky suspected, the NSA.

As with Stuxnet, this malware typically infects a PC via a USB flash drive, and it features an ingenious, self-perpetuating design. With every system boot, the hard drive firmware will reintroduce the malware, even if a user wipes down all files, reformats the drive, and installs a new operating system. The only solution is to replace the hard drive—assuming that one can trust that the new drive does not have the same bug.

Every hard-drive brand, whether Seagate or Western Digital or other brand, has its own unique proprietary and complex firmware, even the simplest of which contains millions of lines of code. Before the hack occurred, it was thought to be impossible to hack even a single manufacturer's firmware code, much less the codes of close to a dozen different drive makers. Manufacturers have denied sharing their firmware codes with any government agency. Regardless, whoever hacked the firmware codes of multiple hard-drive manufacturers made it clear that even low-level components of hard drives are vulnerable to attack.

Such an alleged violation of privacy is too serious to be ignored, but an even greater risk is the injection of malicious code into firmware. The consolidation of disk-drive manufacturers, mentioned earlier, further complicates the matter. The same attack today would only have to target two disk-drive companies, since over 95 percent of all drives used in enterprise storage are manufactured by Seagate Technology and Western Digital. A similar attack of a much smaller magnitude could prove devastating. If, for example, a firmware bug instructed all Seagate drives to crash next Tuesday and for all Western Digital drives to follow the day after, the Internet stops. If all Internet data is stored on magnetic disk, society stops.

The U.S. Power Grid: A Soft Target?

Even the briefest power outage is an inconvenience to most of us, and especially to IT infrastructure managers who go to great lengths to mitigate against power loss with redundant services, huge uninterruptable power supplies (UPS), and backup generators. However, power loss is an inevitable occurrence and could be categorized along with storms and employee misfeasance. A brief, regional power outage requires that plans be in place that will ensure restored service, data protection, and continuity, even if such an outage is more likely to be caused by a squirrel than a terrorist.[15]

Yet a serious assault on the power grids of developed nations is as imaginable as it would be catastrophic. The Ukrainian power grid was brought down in December 2015, and many saw on it the fingerprints of Russian hackers.[16] A March 2015 *USA Today* investigation suggested that an attempt is made to compromise the U.S. power grid every four hours:

> Although the repeated security breaches have never resulted in the type of cascading outage that swept across the Northeast in 2003, they have sharpened concerns about vulnerabilities in the electric system. A widespread outage lasting even a few days could disable devices ranging from ATMs to cellphones to traffic lights, and could threaten lives if heating, air conditioning and health care systems exhaust their backup power supplies.[17]

Many fear that the aging power grid infrastructure in the United States is particularly vulnerable to cyber-attacks. The unthinkable becomes the inevitable when one considers the possibility of extended outages across a large geographic area. Replacing destroyed power transformers could take months, with little chance of accelerating the replacement and with the manufacturing and shipping of required parts being impeded by the same outage that is being addressed.

A high beta event such as a massive failure of the U.S. power grid—indeed all the threats outlined in this book thus far—can understandably instill a sense of futility regarding how digital preservation can be guaranteed under such a severely challenging and seemingly inevitable "disaster" scenario. Planning for routine problems, however, can be amended to provide better preparation for more catastrophic events, and preparing for large events helps ensure continuity during smaller ones.

In many ways the situation today is more promising than ever before. All technologies associated with storage have increased in capacity and decreased in cost. All the storage media discussed in this book, be it solid-state disk, disk, tape, optical, or cloud, have unique strengths and weaknesses. Leveraging them through well-planned, balanced strategies will provide the best defense against any form of cyber-attack, including future attacks enabled by technologies not yet developed or methods that cannot be foreseen. Regardless of how the landscape of data threats changes, maintaining genetic diversity will remain a constant and critical aspect of reliable, long-term data storage.

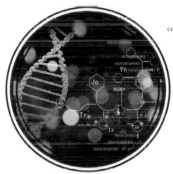

"The genes had found a way to delegate their ambitions, by building bodies capable not just of survival, but of intelligent behavior as well. Now, if a gene found itself in an animal threatened by winter storms, it could rely on its body to do something clever like migrate south or build itself a shelter."
—Matt Ridley, *Genome: The Autobiography of a Species in 23 Chapters*

Chapter 9

Deep Storage and Genetic Diversity

The many threats discussed in previous chapters can be ranked by severity or probability. Most of them are high-beta events: They are thankfully rare, but nevertheless sufficiently cata- strophic to warrant consideration when designing an approach to long-term digital preservation.

Nassim Nicholas Taleb's books *Antifragile* and *Black Swan* highlight the importance of contouring a risk profile to include black swan events, a term popularized by Taleb and which refers to events that are unpredictable and beyond the norm, yet have a massive impact. Black swan events are not served by conventional planning, which typically includes a risk profile optimized for a normal probability distribution, an example of which in the financial world would be investment in popular index funds.[1] In the world of data storage and preservation, it would cover typical redundancy; specifically, the creation of multiple copies of data kept in disparate geographic locations. In contrast, preparation for a black swan event must be more rigorous and requires adding diversity with the goal of reducing "fragility" (susceptibility to loss).

Consider the genetic differences between the birds discussed in Chapter 1. In the biological world, diversity defeats fragility and can protect a species from the many possible shocks it will face. In the digital world, at least four different types of diversity should be considered when creating a deep-storage data preservation system: diversity of protocol, diversity of media, diversity of volatility, and diversity of geography.

Diversity of Protocol

Many malicious threats target specific access protocols, the most important sets of which are TCP/IP, HTTP, and FTP. For instance, a DDoS attack might use the HTTP protocol, but it would need to be rewritten to affect a network file share and the different security protocols that wrap each share. Just as computer viruses initially target the most popular operating systems and corporate tool components, malicious attacks at data "go where the money is," targeting well-known, standard-access protocols.

HTTP and FTP are widely used protocols that provide immediate, live access to online resources. The networked, online file-system protocols of traditional network protocols have generally been of greater use on internal networks and inside virtual private networks (VPN). The expanded use of open-source HADOOP software and the growing popularity of cloud storage come with increased convenience, but also with potential vulnerabilities.

Object-oriented, deferred storage application program interfaces (API) like Amazon S3 and Spectra Logic S3 offer object-centered storage on cloud or internal networks accessible by REST-based (Representational State Transfer) Web services. If the underlying disk or tape storage media is the

Fig. 1 Amazon's S3 interface is a classic example of a "RESTful" API used to interface with object or cloud storage. Many manufacturers offer object storage interfaces similar to the command set found in S3.

same, and susceptible to some of the same risks, then establishing a diversity in access methods can shield a company against certain attacks aimed at direct-access storage.

The real question, however, is not about figuring out which protocol is generally "safer," but about how to best create diversity so that a single threat does not endanger multiple data repositories. In this regard, diversity of protocol is one important way of making it difficult to damage every copy of the data through a single attack.

Diversity of Media Types

As discussed in Chapter 1, consolidation in the storage industry has brought with it many benefits. Storage is currently cheaper than many of the most optimistic projections predicted that it would be, and the standards in form factor and platform protocols have simplified data management, purchasing, and systems design. Yet decreasing diversity has also brought about the problem of fragility. Out of the more than 70 manufacturers of tape and disk drives that were active in the 1980s and 1990s, only a few remain. Fewer manufacturers and greater reliance on common standards mean that a firmware defect, malicious code, or direct attack in a protocol or device driver could potentially wreak havoc—even over a wide geographic area and across different functionalities.

Diversity of media should be considered as a counterbalance to consolidation onto a single media or platform because it is the easiest and most effective way to introduce or strengthen overall genetic diversity in data storage. A complete copy of primary disk data stored on a secondary disk (preferably using a different storage protocol), tape, or optical media offers the best chance of data survival against malicious threats or human error.

Google's Raymond Blum put it most directly when explaining why his company uses tape for archiving: "Tape is great because it is not disk."[2] The same diversity argument applies to flash or optical storage media, as well as to any future storage medium, be it cartridges of optical panels, holographic media, or even biological storage in DNA. The best practice is to always use at least two media types so that the entirety of an organization's data is not susceptible to a single threat.

In addition to being practical, media used for archiving needs to meet durability and restorability requirements. Media that is expensive or difficult to obtain will not support a long-term strategy. Drives that are expensive or hard to maintain, or media that is difficult to store and ship, will not make for pleasant budget meeting discussions throughout the decades of their deployment.

Fig. 2 Each storage media type has specific strengths and weaknesses, but different media used together can optimize storage performance, costs, and reliability while improving diversity.

It is equally important to consider the expected life cycles of media and reading/recording devices. Disk drives have a typical life expectancy of three years, while the life cycle of tape drives tends to be closer to eight years. Although optical drives do have a shorter life expectancy, their cost is significantly lower. And so, there are many ways to arrive at a total cost when considering a multiyear or multidecade storage approach.

Although there might not be shelves empty of disk drives at present, should scarcity of storage media become a reality, it would be very disruptive to projected market prices. Sites that rely on multiple platforms, media, and technologies would have an advantage here, since they can simply reapportion storage across different media types as prices change. If all storage and archive data rest on a single medium, price volatility is potentially detrimental. By having more media types in the mix, the percentage of each type can be adjusted to provide the best cost per zettabyte. Most data centers are already using multiple media formats as part of their archival rotation. These savvy planners achieve genetic diversity by altering procedures and updating equipment.

Diversity of Volatility

Digital preservation professionals talk about the importance of maintaining an "air gap" for at least some components of a storage system. For example, an EMP attack can threaten everything nearby and a catastrophic power surge can destroy everything attached to power and data ports. In cases such as these, data that has been stored far from the disaster event, or is offline, has the best chance of survival. Tape and optical storage media, specifically, have built-in air gaps and have historically been the preferred options for offsite, nonvolatile storage. Flash or magnetic disk media can also serve as nonvolatile storage options, but their use would require procedural changes to provide protection from online threats; air gaps must be consciously inserted by keeping some media offline.

Regardless of where it is stored—in a bunker or a closet—online data is exposed to more threats than offline media. Therefore, procedures and solutions that allow the rapid copy of current transaction data to offline storage will lessen the risk for data loss due to a malicious attempt to delete or overwrite. Optical storage, being intrinsically write once, read many, is a good choice for this, followed by offline, vaulted tape, and then by object storage, such as Amazon S3 and Spectra S3. Online, immediate access is certainly required for transactional applications, however the data's distance from the network (geographic or chronologic) can offer protection for archival storage.

Combining a tiered storage environment that can quickly move copies to offline media together with robust procedures to disperse that media is a solid approach to protecting data from catastrophic events. Mirroring, or quickly migrating data to a geographically diverse site, places a smaller portion of the new data at risk. Many firms rely on a super-redundancy method of storing many copies in the cloud. This might overcome many threats, but the strategy of keeping all valuable data online lacks both diversity of volatility and diversity of media types. On some level all online data must be thought of as being vulnerable. To ensure its survival, an organization must keep sufficient copies of its genome offline.

Conducting due diligence on a specific cloud provider's diversity is also well warranted. To deal with a true catastrophe, most firms will elect to keep a copy of their genome under their direct control, both to ensure data preservation and to reduce restoration time after a major event. During a serious crisis, it is likely that bandwidth will be scarce and that other cloud customers might be in line ahead of you. Time-sensitive restoration efforts will benefit from local data. It is also important to consider the viability of the cost associated with relying on the cloud for large, disaster recovery.

Since the upload to the cloud usually trickles over time, the cost of a one-time restoration of all data can be prohibitive.

Diversity of Geography

Superstorm Sandy, discussed in Chapter 5, devastated a large, populous, and data-dense geographic area. Doubtless, the disaster-recovery plans of many organizations in the affected areas probably involved storing data at two locations instead of one—a good idea on paper, but without a sizable geographic separation, a single event can threaten both preservation sites. Diversity in geography calls for the consideration of several factors. First, although bandwidth has improved, it is rarely sufficient to transfer all the data requiring protection from one location to another without having to physically ship equipment itself. Professor of computer science and author Andrew Tanenbaum once quipped, "Never underestimate the bandwidth of a station wagon full of tapes rolling down the Interstate."[3] Or as Randall Munroe, author of *What If?* quotes Johan Öbrink, "When—if ever—will the bandwidth of the Internet surpass that of FedEx?"[4]

When choosing to diversify, details matter. Media type, storage, weight, retrieval time, and shipping costs deserve the same consideration as is given to capacity and throughput. High-beta event preparations need to be cost effective, accounting for not only the acquisition of systems, but also media replacement, storage, shipping, and maintenance. It should be kept in mind, however, that diversity that doubles costs will not survive more than a few budget cycles, much less a flood.

Cloud storage is a convenient way to establish a diversity of geography, but as a means of digital preservation—that is, the survival of an organization's genome—it is generally insufficient. This makes it all the more critical to know what methods providers are using to ensure data survival, and then to factor that information into a diversity matrix. Paramount is recognizing that the ultimate responsibility for recovery should not be outsourced to another firm without a clear understanding of the restoration cost, coverage, and time required.

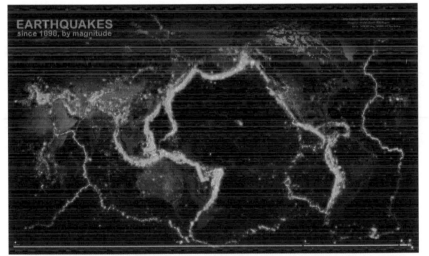

Fig. 3 This 2012 map, created by cartographer and user-experience designer John Nelson, depicts every earthquake recorded at a magnitude of 4.0 or higher. It is a compelling reason for establishing diversity of geography.

It also bears noting that, although ensuring diversity of geography might be the most important precaution to take for natural and man-made catastrophes, it will not protect against every scenario, such as a threat that compromises multiple data locations simultaneously. And diversity of geography might not be as robust as it could be if all an organization's data is kept under

137

the wing of a single provider, for even providers with the best procedures in place can become targets for malicious attacks. For this and other reasons, no IT department, much less its organization, would appreciate having to rely on a single source for any important product or service. Maintaining local copies of important data does have its advantages, such as being able to change vendors if necessary and to control restoration.

Finally, there will always be a situation for which diversity of geography has no practical significance. Take the example of one business that stores multiple copies of its data in two locations that are only six blocks apart in a modern urban area. When pressed about the need for "tectonic separation," the customer admitted that should the six city blocks that his local business served be destroyed, there would be no business remaining to warrant a restoration. It was not that a greater disaster was not contemplated; instead, a conscious decision was made to align the level of preservation needed with the organization's geographic aegis.

The Diversity End Game

True genetic diversity requires paying attention to common threats. A flood can damage both an online disk and the box of tapes stacked up in the corner of the data center. A coordinated attack could target data centers in both Mumbai and Cleveland. At their base, most digital preservation strategies are extensions of the best IT practices, but ensuring the survival of an organization's genome also requires a few counterintuitive methods and the willingness to recognize the possibility of unconventional and catastrophic threats.

An extended power outage is perhaps the most commonly imagined of unthinkable threats. Data retrieval might not be the first concern, but restoring systems will likely be the first step toward restoring modernity. This is especially true for whoever is responsible for restoring the grid or a power station, or for manufacturing components required for recovery. Mapping out a recovery strategy is a good exercise in diversity.

In the case of an unexpected and extended outage, there is a high likelihood of data loss on main storage systems, and therefore data will likely have to be restored from another copy. In a simple mirroring scenario, if one data center lies beyond the geographic range of the outage, nothing is lost but transitory data not yet mirrored. However, if the outage affects all data centers containing unique data, that data will have to be restored to equipment located outside the affected area. Tape or optical media is the easiest to ship. Archives already stored at a safe site or in a vault are best positioned to facilitate recovery. Diversity of protocol, of media, of volatility, and of geography will all contribute to a successful recovery.

Best storage practices and methods aside, what does catastrophic data loss mean in the grand scheme of things? How could society's genome be compromised? Through books and movies, research and debates, and everyday meetings and conversations, we are presented with endless visions of a future world in which modern civilization has been derailed and set back to zero. Just how close to such a cataclysmic reality can we get?

Perhaps no one will be fired for losing last month's commission spreadsheet due to an EMI attack. But should agricultural firms lose track of their seed stock or pharmaceuticals lose the ability to manufacture, then the lives of people around the world can be threatened. A quick literature search will yield countless stories and statistics of corporations that struggled with, or failed to survive, catastrophic data loss, although better hardware and practices have made these events less common, especially for the typical threats of hardware failure, human error, and software defects. By extending best practices and attention to diversity, in the here and now, we can provide similar protection from less commonly occurring yet still high-risk events.

More important and far-reaching, however, is our effort to protect society's genome by making genetic diversity the cornerstone of a robust digital preservation strategy, one that allows organizations to withstand real-world threats as well as leverage future technological advancements. In its final chapter, *Society's Genome* offers practical data preservation take-aways for achieving these goals through its "Seven Tenets of Good Archiving."

"In God we trust. All others must bring data."
—W. Edwards Deming

Chapter 10

Digital Preservation

At its most basic level, preserving an organization's genome entails executing most of the mundane backup and best archival practices that every competent IT shop is performing. However, ensuring long-term evolutionary survival requires adding on a few more critical procedures and policies to create an efficient data archival workflow. And before that can be established, one must first go down a digital checklist to determine priorities and options, including assessing the purpose of the data, identifying the data that is or is not valuable to the genome, and weighing the pros and cons of data preservation methods—costs in particular—against these and other goals.

Curation for the purposes of preservation is essentially not unlike taking realistic stock of our personal belongings. Who has not asked themselves at some point in time, "Will I really ever wear that old sweater again?" An organizational equivalent could be, "How long are you going to keep the meeting minutes from last year's planning meeting?" Chapter 3 introduced Sydney Brenner's distinction between "junk" and "garbage." Brenner's concept is worth revisiting here in a direct excerpt from his 1998 *Current Biology* article:

> Some years ago I noticed that there were two kinds of rubbish in the world and that most languages have different words to distinguish them. There is the rubbish we keep, which is junk, and the rubbish we throw away, which is garbage. The excess DNA in our genomes is junk, and is there because it is harmless, as well as being useless, and because the molecular processes generating extra DNA outpace those getting rid of it. Were the extra DNA to become disadvantageous, it would become subject to selection, just as junk that takes up too much space, or is beginning to smell, is instantly converted garbage.[1]

A good archival workflow must include the task of separating that data which is vital for immediate retrieval from junk data that might have value for future analytics or Big Data analysis. Junk data can then be stored on another data tier. True garbage data—whether completely worthless or potentially harmful in litigation—should be put out on the metaphorical curb.

The development of a data archival workflow is highly specific to each organization; however, it should account for target utilization, budget, and regulatory compliance requirements. Also common to all workflow plans is the need to define how long data should be kept, how quickly it may need to be accessed in the future, and the level of protection that it requires from high-beta threats.

As more and more data is computationally generated instead of merely collected, organizations will often wonder whether they should preserve the generated data set. Given the current curve of increasing computational power, it would be prudent to store the (far smaller) algorithm then regenerate the data on more powerful future computers if needed. The decision to adopt this expedient lies with each organization, but it might be worth the effort. Many scientific firms, for example, have found meaningful defects in their generated data. By definition, their results would be difficult if not impossible to reproduce if the compromised data set were unavailable for comparison. For organizations that aggressively prune data, the random preservation of a large data set might be difficult to justify. Regardless, the decision to allow data to expire and become permanently unavailable should never be made without first accurately assessing the data's potential value.

Different types of data users (outlined in Chapter 4) require different procedures and workflows, and while a detailed discussion of these approaches lies outside the scope of this book, what has been emphasized throughout it is the critical importance of enforcing deep-storage and genetic diversity and applying the best IT backup and archival practices to digital preservation—all of which can increase the likelihood of an organization's genome surviving catastrophic events.

When conceiving a data preservation plan, it always helps to examine how other organizations have implemented robust workflows and procedures. One particular category of data users worth watching closely are organizations that operate in the curation and preservation vertical markets, and which have developed and formalized many innovative digital preservation strategies. Although not all aspects of their rigorous approaches will fit into a typical corporate backup plan, their methods are nevertheless worth investigating. The following organizations in particular have produced well-considered plans and have made many facets of these plans public:

- USC SHOAH Foundation (http://sfi.usc.edu/)
- Wikipedia Digital Preservation
  (https://en.wikipedia.org/wiki/Digital_ preservation)
- Library of Congress (www.loc.gov)
- National Archives and Records Administration
  (www.archives.gov)
- Church of Jesus Christ of Latter-Day Saints
  (www.lds.org)
- Storage Networking Industry Association
  (www.snia.org)
- Society of Motion Picture & Television Engineers
  (www.smpte.org)

Backups Are Not Archives

A storage workflow needs to carefully distinguish between what constitutes a data backup and a data archive. There is some functional overlap between the two, but conflating them can lead to restoration problems. Archived data typically does not change, and the cleanest example of this data category is found in the media and entertainment vertical. For instance, in the case of a completed film project, for which the prints have already been shipped or the content has already aired, there is generally no need to again access or re-edit the materials. All the project data can be written to media (to two types in tectonically separated locations, of course), where it can remain until if and when it is needed, such as for a film sequel or retrospective.

In 2009, 20th Century Fox's film *Avatar* was rendered in about one petabyte of CGI (computer-generated imagery) and digitized film data, using a 100-node supercomputer.[2] All that data clearly needs to be readily available from the studio's archive when needed, but day-to-day uses would likely require only metadata and moderate-resolution files of post-rendered images. To support a sequel (no, the authors have no inside knowledge) or remastered anniversary release project, a test restoration of the data would have to be conducted months in advance.

A film project is an easy example here because the data is already known to be of high value, the end of mutability is clearly determined, and all the project's components can be captured during a single production cycle. But the more common reality is that data remains in flux with a more ambiguous retention value, and components can change at any time. Similar procedures might apply, albeit with more arbitrary completion schedules. For example, financial data might be archived after the fiscal year closes or an audit is completed.

Fig. 1 A movie re-release is a classic example of monetizing data over decades. *Gone With the Wind* has had eight U.S. re-releases since 1939, earning it over $400 million ($3 to $5 billion adjusted for inflation) and making it the all-time highest-grossing movie.[3]

The temptation here would be to treat backups as archived media. If a backup of the financials was run the night of the audit, one might call it lunchtime and assume there is no more to be done. However the life cycle of a proper archive requires different handling because while the data of an archive does not change, its digital preservation is a living, breathing, forward-moving object. Nightly backups may take snapshots of changing data, but backups are still essentially static. Last night's backup could be overwritten or discarded within a relatively short time period. If new drives are not backward compatible, some of the old equipment will have to remain online until a complete set of new backups is created.

In contrast, a true archive is routinely rewritten to include new media and current formats. The unfortunate reality is that, if presented with a box of 10- or 15-year-old backups, most organizations would struggle to restore even a portion of them. This is why it is important to view archives as living entities that require ongoing attention and care. Soon after an organization adopts a new storage technology, it should move its archives forward onto the new technology, so that the formats are never multiple hops behind the tools being used to retrieve them.

But Are Archives Backups?

Day-to-day backups have been evolving in character, with some organizations backing up less often and concentrating more on archival storage. Enterprise RAID (redundant array of independent disks), real-time mirroring, transactional logging, and an increased use of versioning platforms have obviated many of the traditional reasons for backup. If yesterday's "good version" of the spreadsheet is on a browser-based collaboration platform such as SharePoint, the enterprise resource planning (ERP) system can be rolled back. This makes data loss to hardware failure a $1:10^{10}$ risk, diminishing the reasons for traditional backup. It should be noted, however, that backups can lessen the amount of data that is at risk at a given time, as well as allow an IT organization to offer more full-featured restoration services.

Each organization must decide for itself whether archives can fulfill the needs of backup (while still bearing in mind that expecting backups to function as archives ignores several important process requirements).

The Seven Tenets of Good Archiving

The following seven tenets of good archiving, published by Spectra Logic Corporation, reflect a robust approach to digital preservation that can guide organizations in leveraging together best IT practices and the principles of maintaining genetic diversity.

Tenet 1: Open standards

Workflows should support the promotion of archived data to new media and current formats. Long-term archive media should exceed their advertised life-spans in case the data or content are needed long after initially estimated. The best way to ensure restorability is have it written in a standardized and nonproprietary format. Other formats could be considered appropriate for general storage if they truly offer advantages, but since long-term archives are a time capsule for the future, they require standard physical formats, protocols, and input points that are open, published, and well defined. The client-server file system NFS (network file system), for example, is an open standard supported by more than 100 vendors.

Tenet 2: Metadata preservation

Metadata, or the data that describes the data, is extremely small in comparison to an actual data set. Although its marginal value is great, metadata is increasingly being omitted from the actual file. Content management systems (CMS) frequently generate or manage extended information, including author and versioning information, as well as tagging, descriptions, and relationships to products or projects. Metadata should be generated at the time of data creation or importation into the CMS, since there is little possibility, or willingness, to retroactively add this descriptive data. Ensuring that metadata is saved so that it can be linked to the appropriate files or data requires additional planning and testing in a restoration scenario.

Tenet 3: Forward migration

Digital assets must always be migrated forward onto new media and formats. Some media types are more volatile than others with respect to their physical formats and specifications, and all have varied life-spans. Optical media is well positioned for long-term storage, while solid-state drives have a shorter yet durable life-span. Even magnetic tape, which is the standard for long-term storage, requires occasional re-tensioning. New formats, however, always offer performance benefits and easier access. Migrating forward to new technology every three to eight years is worthwhile; however, migration is ideally driven by the adoption of new formats. Archive media should never be more than one generation old, and devices that can read it must be readily available. (A number of YouTube clips show young people trying to figure out how to use "old" technology, such as a Sony Walkman tape player or a 1980s-era desktop computer. Although amusing to watch, they nevertheless speak strongly to the truth of how rapidly today's cutting-edge formats can become obsolete.)

Tenet 4: Multiple copies of the data

Redundancy alone is not the ultimate solution to data archiving, but without it there is no diversity, which starts with having at least two pieces of media. Even long-term archival storage via NFS requires a second copy of the data should the first copy fail to read.

Tenet 5: Tectonic separation

The principle of tectonic separation, also referred to as geographic diversity or geographic separation, is key to creating a resilient multiple-copy archive. All copies of data should be physically separated from each other. If all data sets can be destroyed by a single event, then the separation is not great enough.

A favorite solution for geographic diversity is cloud storage. Before an organization moves its data to the cloud, however, it is important to verify just how much diversity it will have. Choosing a single endpoint provides multiple copies on a cluster—a good move. But the copies are then often stored within a single-mile radius. This could afford protection from a fire, but perhaps not from an earthquake or hurricane. The tradeoff is clear: It costs more to opt for multiple data centers, but multiple data centers can provide more protection. Likewise, using cloud data centers located in two West Coast states is better than relying on a single endpoint. Better still would be to store data on the West Coast and somewhere in Europe—although it would be more expensive.

Important to note is that redundancy among multiple data centers is by demand only and typically requires a substantive upcharge. An alternative is to use an in-house "private cloud" and to store all archive data copies in a remote "public cloud" location or on tape that is shipped far away. This would provide diversity in protocol, vendor, and media with a concomitantly higher chance of data survival.

Cloud storage is an excellent item in the diversity toolkit, and premier providers of this space can offer robust and well-planned digital preservation procedures and equipment. Augmenting this type of storage by maintaining data copies under your organization's control increases protection and improves restoration options. Conversely, organizations that do not use cloud storage need to emulate the protections that cloud storage offers in terms of redundancy and geographic diversity. Although the initial investment of this approach can be higher, the cost over the long term is often lower.

Tenet 6: Fingerprint of the data set

Establishing a method to verify your data at any given juncture is an important component of any data archival workflow. An MD5 checksum, or similar "fingerprint" of a data set, ensures that the data being pulled out of an archive is the same data that was put into it. A checksum is a small (16- to 512-bit) value that has been computed from an entire file or archive, irrespective of the source's length. A good checksum or hash algorithm will produce a different value with even a small change in the input data set.

The fingerprint analogy is apt because the small value is unique and can be used to tell different files apart from each other. Ideally, an organization would run the checksum when the file is first stored, then store the checksum. When the file is subsequently transferred, compressed, encrypted, or restored, the checksum is once again computed to determine if there is a match (or "collision").

Among their many applications, including identifying possibly corrupt files, checksums are used extensively for security and encryption, for which more sophisticated algorithms are continually released to stay ahead of purposeful exploitation. Cyclic Redundancy Check (CRC), developed in 1961, and a slightly expanded CRC32 are still used to check data integrity of compressed ZIP files, but their use in security or cryptography applications is strongly discouraged. More powerful computers enable the use of more sophisticated algorithms, but, of course, this same power could become available to those who attempt unauthorized access.

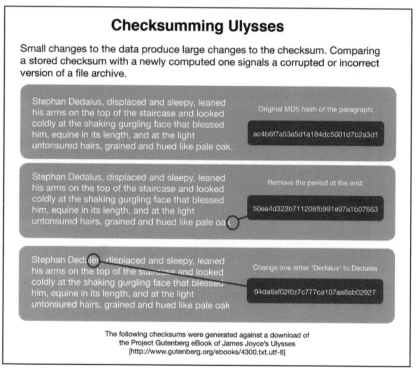

Checksumming Ulysses

Small changes to the data produce large changes to the checksum. Comparing a stored checksum with a newly computed one signals a corrupted or incorrect version of a file archive.

Stephan Dedalus, displaced and sleepy, leaned his arms on the top of the staircase and looked coldly at the shaking gurgling face that blessed him, equine in its length, and at the light untonsured hairs, grained and hued like pale oak.

Original MD5 hash of the paragraph:

ac4b6f7a53a5d1a184dc5001d7b2a3d1

Stephan Dedalus, displaced and sleepy, leaned his arms on the top of the staircase and looked coldly at the shaking gurgling face that blessed him, equine in its length, and at the light untonsured hairs, grained and hued like pale oa

Remove the period at the end:

50ea4d323b711208fb991e97a1b07663

Stephan Dedales, displaced and sleepy, leaned his arms on the top of the staircase and looked coldly at the shaking gurgling face that blessed him, equine in its length, and at the light untonsured hairs, grained and hued like pale oak

Change one letter 'Dedalus' to Dedales

94da8af02f0z7c777ca107aa8ab02927

The following checksums were generated against a download of the Project Gutenberg eBook of James Joyce's Ulysses [http://www.gutenberg.org/ebooks/4300.txt.utf-8]

Fig. 2 A checksum is a simple but effective error-detection method for ensuring the integrity of data that has been stored or is transmitted.

Modern algorithms like MD5, SHA-1, SHA-256, SHA-512 are larger and have more difficulty creating a purposeful match. Using them provides a marginal improvement in checking data integrity, as there is even less of a chance of having any corruption escape detection. However, the true value of these algorithms lies in the protection that they afford from a deliberate breach, such as an attempt to maliciously replace a file in an archive and match the checksum. For general purposes, any common checksum method will suffice. The worst choice is to use no fingerprinting method at all.

Error checking also has parallels in genetic systems. When cells reproduce, several proteins perform a process analogous to a data center's checksum to ascertain exact replication of an organism's genome. The integrity of the genetic information is verified during cell division, and proteins such as p53 can stop replication and activate either a DNA repair or a cell-death program if significant DNA damage is detected. Perhaps, if the genetic toolbox had checksumming as accurate as SHA-256, cancer and other diseases might be far less common.

As with metadata, capturing these digital fingerprints and using them to proof restoration is imperative for successful long-term data preservation. Knowing that the data has changed allows for data recovery from a second copy, but, just as important, digital fingerprints can also confirm that data has remained exactly the same over time—in other words, that no one has tampered with it. This is especially critical for organizations that deal with scientific, medical, or financial data, where pulling incorrect data could have significant ramifications.

Tenet 7: Genetic diversity

Genetic diversity requires that all of an organization's data not be moved through or stored on a single type of system. Firmware, hardware, or software defects can compromise or delete data just as easily as can human error or cyber-attacks. Having data travel through and onto two different endpoint devices that use different technologies can help prevent a system defect from destroying data.

Chapter 9 describes at length the different levels of diversity to consider, with the central idea being that one event— whatever its cause—should not deny access to a large portion of an organization's data. J. P. Morgan said (perhaps apocryphally), "Put all your eggs in one basket—and watch the basket!" Morgan was a great innovator in the financial sphere, but this is terrible advice for IT professionals.

Continuing the Conversation

This book has presented the highs and lows of life in our digital universe—from the excitement and promise of the Digital Revolution to the significant threats posed by cybercriminals to the practical approaches necessary for maintaining the growth and security of society's genome. We hope that you as a reader will walk away with a sense of optimism for today's world as well as for the future world that we are building.

Some of the ideas presented in this book may be new to you, but none should seem out of line with common sense. Even having no knowledge of genetics, Queen Victoria was wise enough to theorize the dangers of limited diversity, writing to her daughter Vicky, "I do wish one could find some more black-eyed Princes and Princesses for our children!... For that constant fair hair and blue eyes makes the blood so lymphatic...."[4]

The understanding that we have today of cause and effect has come a long way since the days of potato blight and cousin marriage. One must also acknowledge, however, that the knowledge and understanding of the 1800s was nevertheless more extensive than that of previous centuries. A given society does not, in general, develop insights spontaneously in a vacuum. Each new generation stands upon the shoulders of previous generations, and this simple fact underscores how essential it is that the great breadth and depth of humankind's collective knowledge be passed on to those who will continue to explore it and add to it their own legacies.

In that spirit, *Society's Genome* is intended to serve not as a summary, but as a spark for continuing the conversation. What new forms of technology hold the greatest promise for digital preservation? Which older forms of technology will find new life and purpose and which will cease to be? While these and other questions are timely and relevant, we must also not focus solely on the future and the solutions that might come. We must commit to applying the principle of genetic diversity to the data systems of today, for failing to do so puts society's genome at risk.

One of the easiest areas in which to implement genetic diversity is in the choice of the media used to store data or digital content. Recognizing that flash, disk, tape, and other storage media technologies advance rapidly, Spectra has published an analysis of the industry's current media types that also includes projections on future capacities, performance, availability, and cost. "Outlook for Data Storage," found in the appendix of this book, provides an overview of this analysis and is highly recommended reading for anyone who is interested in introducing genetic diversity to their data storage system using current and projected future storage technologies. (The original white paper, *Digital Data Storage Outlook 2016,* which is referenced in the appendix is available at www.spectralogic.com and will be updated yearly.) We welcome suggestions from other industry participants and users on this material.

Agree or disagree with any premises presented in this book? We would love to hear your thoughts and ideas. Updates to *Society's Genome* will be published on the book's website www.societysgenome.com, which includes an open forum for comments and discussion, as well as bibliographic information, examples of innovative digital preservation strategies, and other useful information.

It is our hope that in addition to providing practical guidance and insights on best protecting and preserving your organization's data for the future, this book has prompted you to further ponder the importance of propagating society's genome.

Acknowledgments

The authors would like to thank the innumerable friends and coworkers who contributed valuable ideas and counsel to this project; most notably, David Trachy, for his industry research, and Matt Starr, for the "Seven Tenets of Good Archiving" in Chapter 10.

Special thanks go to Kristen Coats for graphic design; to Eric Polet for charts, graphs, and tables; to Tanner Greer for his editing and research assistance; and to Tracy Kendall for developing the *Society's Genome* website (www.societysgenome.com). To Susan Merriman for her individual contributions, as well as managing the overall effort, thank you.

Special acknowledgment goes to Mary Kalamaras for her unwavering guidance and dedication to the editing and research that helped us bring this book into being.

Appendix
Outlook for Data Storage

Society's Genome explores the modern world's explosive data growth and the importance of preserving the unprecedented amount of information being created. One of the most important factors that must be considered in this new digital reality is whether media production will keep pace with demand. Secure long-term preservation of digital assets requires no fewer than two copies, likely more. If data growth continues at its present levels, will there be enough media to store it? More practically speaking, what roles will scarcity and affordability play in media choice?

Establishing a baseline for future storage needs requires examining both the historical and current trends that have thus far driven digital storage use. While manufacturers do offer their own expectations of future media supply, such projections are not enough given the factors at play, some of which are as yet unknown. For its part, Spectra Logic has factored in several additional considerations, described below, to provide a more comprehensive assessment of trends in media technologies, including their capacities, performance, pricing, and availability.

Storage History

The human genome has no knowledge of the future, but it does have, as British science journalist Matt Ridley points out, "unrivalled access to information about the past."[1] Likewise, the history of data storage provides a foundation for predicting future procedures, methods, and technologies. Advances in storage have been as remarkable as advances made in microprocessors, and are far more visible.

The history of modern data storage all began with holes in paper, a technology used even before computing. Player-piano rolls stored event data for machine reading, in what could be considered a forerunner to the modern MIDI (musical instrument digital interface) standard. Individuals who stored programs on rolls of paper tape or IBM punch cards might now regard 256-gigabyte USB thumb drives with a special sense of wonder, or as witchcraft. The practice of storing data by magnetizing a section of wire, drum, tape, or the platter of a disk drive followed soon thereafter, but at high cost and in unwieldy formats. Yet most of today's data is still being stored using the same methods, just in orders of magnitude greater in areal densities.

Beyond physical holes or magnetized particles is another medium for storing data—the use of reflected or refracted light. Optical media storage has historically dominated the consumer sector for data publishing and distribution, and to some extent data storage. Optical media has several unique features, as well as a few limitations and challenges that will be discussed later.

NAND flash media is a solid-state technology that offers access times in the same neighborhood as system RAM but without the volatility. Flash rose to success in the consumer sector by being the only choice for smaller, more power-efficient music players and digital cameras. Smartphones and tablets now use flash for main storage and, as its cost dropped, flash has also found its way into laptop computers.

In short, the three currently viable methods for storing data, and the way in which all common media types work, is by:

- orienting particles magnetically (disk and tape);
- altering the reflection or refraction of light (optical); and
- capturing electrons (solid-state/DRAM/flash).

This is not to say that other forms of data storage do not exist or are not viable. For example, phase change memory alters the crystalline structure of nonvolatile memory and promises substantive speed improvements in random access.[2] Memristors, or resistive RAM (RRAM), exploit imperfect contacts between nonconducting surfaces.[3] And, fittingly for the title of this book, there have even been laboratory successes with encoding data into DNA.[4] If this method is successfully commercialized, the phrase "worm drive" might soon conjure up an entirely new meaning.

Baseball Hall-of-Famer Yogi Berra once said, "It's tough to make predictions, especially about the future." But barring an unexpected breakthrough, the next decade and beyond will more than likely see the incremental evolution of existing media types. Yes, they will be better, faster, and denser, but they will not fundamentally differ from today's offerings.

Storage Demand

Some people might suppose that population growth would be the strongest factor driving data growth. But it is instead the creation of new applications in the developed world and the spread of technology to the developing world, and there is little in the trend line to suggest a distinct slowdown. Quite a few estimates show growth curves continuing at near current trends. A frequently quoted 2012 IDC report, commissioned by EMC Corporation, projects more than 40 zettabytes generated by 2020, an amount based on current growth trends and increased data creation stemming from new applications and Internet of Things devices.

However, before one places an order for 4,294,967,296 10-terabyte tape cartridges to back up all this data, it must be understood that even if these aggressive predictions come true, a large portion of the data will be transient data with zero, or a very short, planned retention time. Test sensors, surveillance video, and voice data may not even be stored, much less archived with an expectation of future retrieval.

For many organizations, a project can generate quite a bit of data that has no future value. Many digital photos, for example, are discarded after the "keepers" are selected. Audio and video recordings can include outtakes as well gigabytes' worth of sound-level tests and break times. The text for this book was autosaved every 15 minutes with multiple checked-in revisions stored on a corporate server. Only the final manuscript version will be archived for future retrieval. However, the IDC report mentioned above also suggests that 80 percent of this created data will be kept, in what is perhaps its most aggressive prediction.

Nevertheless, despite the immense amount of data at play, storage demand will be tempered by yet another factor: economic concerns. Constraints in storage budgets can force further reductions in the amount of storage that falls under management, although retention needs should continue to warrant economic justification.

Storage Supply

To be sure, society's genome is growing, but based on its own research on how much data will be retained, Spectra Logic predicts that it will not grow to 40 zettabytes by 2020. Rather, more modest growth is anticipated in both the data to be preserved and the storage media required for actually storing that desired data. Holding on to HD surveillance footage to someday track the shopping habits of men wearing blue shirts might have a constituency, but such a justification might be stiffly opposed in the quarterly budget cycle.

The Big Data mantra "keep everything" relies on economic projections for storage costs that might not be reached. The growth of stored data is a product of the data being generated, of what one wants to keep, and of what is economically feasible to store. These three factors can reduce overall predictions without necessarily contradicting them.

Spectra Logic's white paper, *Digital Data Storage Outlook 2016*, includes an examination of current media sales as reported by the manufacturers as a baseline for consumption. Considering the limitation of an assumed mean 5-percent growth for IT spending as well as capacity growth from the published product roadmaps for those same media technologies, Spectra Logic predicts a constrained compound annual growth rate (CAGR) through 2020 and also projects a growth of society's genome by 17 to 20 zettabytes by 2025 (Figure 1).

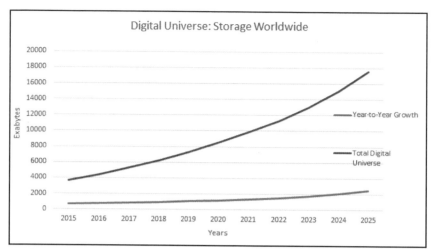

Fig. 1 Spectra Logic predicts a society's genome size in the range of 17 to 20 zettabytes by 2025.

Will There Be Sufficient Media?

While Spectra Logic's estimate is more conservative than other estimates of the total amount of data that will be under management, it is nevertheless a vast amount. If you double it to ensure two copies and also consider that older copies will need to be migrated onto newer formats, then the actual total manufactured storage capacity will need to be far larger to accommodate demand. Many industry insiders and analysts have asked whether manufacturing will be able to keep up, especially if demand comes out on the high side. If one considers only that data for which storage is required, and assuming that technology advances along the lines of manufacturers' published expectations, it appears that capacity projections could keep pace with demand, and so the frequently projected "media gap" seems unlikely.

Yet fear and worry remain, as historically they always have in matters of global supply and demand. In 1798, English cleric and scholar Thomas Robert Malthus predicted widespread famine and disease in *An Essay on the Principle of Population*,[5] warning that the world population, then hovering near one billion, would double every 25 years and outpace food production. In the centuries since this grim yet flawed forecast was made, there have been more predictions of Malthusian catastrophes than any examples of their having come true. Applied to data storage one could warn that the continual extrapolation of falling prices and rising capacities of data storage media might not be sustained at their current rates, but shortages or even rising costs seem unlikely.

The bigger question is, what do differential trends in pricing portend for both storage allocation and storage application? The largest demand, by far, is for immediate online access to data, which is predominantly stored on magnetic disk. Cloud providers are defining storage tiers by price, and the cost of making data immediately accessible might result in some lesser-used data being pushed onto other formats, both in enterprise and cloud storage venues. It might become too costly to have last year's vacation videos—in glorious 4K, of course—made available in seconds. The bottom line is that economic considerations, more than scarcity concerns, will drive the choice to use inexpensive media and to migrate data onto it more quickly.

New Storage Tiers

Managing such large volumes of future data will require apportioning it among multiple media tiers. Increasingly, enterprise data will be stored using technology commensurate with cost, time to access, and application. Just as no one wants to work on a spreadsheet stored on tape because it would take too long to access, flash and magnetic disk are not convenient or economical to ship offsite for disaster recovery.

The traditional function of storage tiers has been time-based: Create a document on your laptop's SSD (tier 1) while on an airplane and upload a copy from your hotel room to your corporate network, where it will likely be stored on enterprise disk (tier 2), backed up to a tape library (tier 3), and eventually archived offsite on tape or optical media (tier 4). Although this process appears tidy, a more holistic and proactive consideration of storage tiers can both improve data safety and save money by directing data to appropriate tiers.

The image of Harriet (Figure 2) provides a great example of tiered storage use as relates to the photo-processing sector. Today, thanks to advances in digital photography, high-resolution images are taking up quite a bit of disk space, aided by the freedom to take essentially unlimited images for free. Cloud services that offer processing must store and manage millions of these large files, few of which will be ever be selected for personal prints or for revenue-generating purposes. This is why the full-resolution image file is a perfect candidate for archiving onto disk, optical, or magnetic tape media. The raw data is rarely rewritten and, if edited, the revised version is considered a separate image. To support Web browsing and image searches, a low-resolution thumbnail is created that becomes a part of the metadata. In this way, Web users need not wait for a tape to be loaded for them to browse photos, yet the bulk of storage can reside on more cost-efficient media.

Fig. 2 An example of tier storage workflow for image processing.

Figure 3 shows the use of different media tiers and the technologies used to support the features described. It is worth noting that the multiple tiers are populated fairly quickly. A file does not migrate through states, but is previewed, backed up, and archived shortly after submission. Over time, the more expensive storage can be reclaimed. The photographer writes over the flash card, and the SSD space of the editing bay is reused for the next project. The relatively quick access times of shingled magnetic recording (SMR) disk and tape library storage might be provided for only 90 days or a year, after which a tape would be requested from a vault. In time, the offline tape and the small thumbnail might be the only files kept, but this would be sufficient to support the photo-processing services offered to the user.

Media Tiers

	2016 Technology	2016 Nominal Access	2020 Nominal Access	2016 Price	2020 Price
	SSD	10µs	1µs	$300/TB	$175/TB
	Disk	5ms	5ms	$65/TB	$38/TB
	SMR Disk	15ms*	15ms	$30/TB	$18/TB
	Tape Library	120s	90s	$21/TB**	$5.5/TB**
	Offline	4 hr***	4 hr***	$11/TB	$3/TB

* Access time for SMR drives are equivalent to enterprise disk, but writes may take significantly longer.
** Marginal media and device cost for Spectra TFinity tape library with LTO technology.
*** Human intervention required to mount tape. Four hour is based on cloud offerings. Likely enterprise response is 4-48 hr.

Fig. 3 Media tier use and technologies.

Enterprise Media Tiers

When considering enterprise media tiers, price and performance are obvious categories used to distinguish among storage options, but application and usage are also important considerations. Relegating data to storage tiers that are less expensive (albeit take longer to access) will play a vital role creating the efficiencies required to store all of society's genome. Through clever caching or aggressive pricing, a significant amount of data can be pushed onto other formats, where it will be available—just not in milliseconds. SSD is ideal for performance-dependent and computational applications and can serve well as a tier for analytics and high-performance computing in the enterprise and cloud-computing sectors. The downside, however, is that SSD costs more and is impractical for long-term storage of large files.

Enterprise disk remains the default medium for current data and will continue to dominate the field in the short term, although other tiers are encroaching. And as unit prices come down, some of the magnetic disk tier will be eclipsed by SSD storage in both enterprise and client applications.

Shingled magnetic recording is an archival magnetic-disk technology that represents a new type of storage tier in that it uses traditional disk form factors, with the difference being that data writes in an overlapping manner, like shingles on a roof. Best performance is achieved by writing data in larger blocks for sequential access, more like magnetic tape. By storing more data on the same disk, the cost per terabyte is reduced, with little or no loss in read-access time. An SMR drive allows for greater density, but it also might slow down the writing process and not use space efficiently if files are frequently overwritten. And while SMR specifications are the same as for standard magnetic disks, the patterns of use differ since SMR is optimized for storing data that will not change. When used appropriately, the rapid access afforded by SMR has made it a medium of choice for many archive applications.

Offline optical or tape storage available through automation requires minutes instead of seconds for access. Although a Web user will not wait for data vended from tape after clicking on a link, SMR makes retrieval of archived data viable, provided that clear expectations about storage and updating are documented.

When offline media is stored outside of an automated library or autochanger, or is not managed robotically, human intervention is required to mount the media. In this case, access times could be measured in hours or more. A service level agreement (SLA) typically specifies expected restore times for data stored on offline media outside of an autochanger/library.

As of this writing, current cloud offerings mirror those of the above tiers. This is not to describe how any one specific cloud storage company operates, but such media types and tiers are becoming accepted and are worth consideration in future planning. Automation and caching to abstract access and hide latency from users is very important in managing expectations for data on longer-access time media. Lines will blur, but it is unrealistic to expect that SSD storage will replace magnetic disk in the server and cloud space. Nor is it likely that disk will jump a tier and replace tape; rather, displacement is more likely than replacement. However, a benefit of diversity is having a portfolio of storage solutions that can be apportioned to fit trends in technology and costs.

Media buyers have come to enjoy Moore's Law–scale advancements occurring in media technology and pricing. In fact, decreased cost and improved technology together serve as a buffer for IT departments taxed with exponential storage needs. Storage manufacturers publish detailed projections of future product releases to gain and retain acceptance of a certain technology or form factor (Figure 4). The information is public and the industry has been predominantly successful in achieving projected capacities near the projected dates. The projections are likely close enough to see rough trends, with the risk factors well documented to establish concerns. Spectra Logic's forecast on media and storage begins by examining what media providers are telling their customers about future trends.

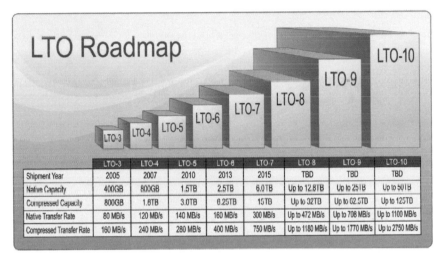

	LTO-3	LTO-4	LTO-5	LTO-6	LTO-7	LTO-8	LTO-9	LTO-10
Shipment Year	2005	2007	2010	2013	2015	TBD	TBD	TBD
Native Capacity	400GB	800GB	1.5TB	2.5TB	6.0TB	Up to 12.8TB	Up to 25TB	Up to 50TB
Compressed Capacity	800GB	1.6TB	3.0TB	6.25TB	15TB	Up to 32TB	Up to 62.5TB	Up to 125TB
Native Transfer Rate	80 MB/s	120 MB/s	140 MB/s	160 MB/s	300 MB/s	Up to 472 MB/s	Up to 708 MB/s	Up to 1100 MB/s
Compressed Transfer Rate	160 MB/s	240 MB/s	280 MB/s	400 MB/s	750 MB/s	Up to 1180 MB/s	Up to 1770 MB/s	Up to 2750 MB/s

Fig. 4 LTO (linear tape-open) data capacity and transfer-rate projections to generation LTO-10.

Magnetic Disk

Magnetic disk has historically been a popular storage medium that has four distinct uses: as client drives for desktops, laptops, and PC backup; as noncompute drives for gaming and DVR consoles; enterprise drives, primarily in  RAID devices both onsite and cloud hosted; and archive drives for storing data in the cloud. Like most manufacturers, disk producers are more concerned with unit volume than with capacity. From a manufacturer's perspective, selling 10,000 two-terabyte disks is much better than selling 5,000 four-terabyte disks even though the total capacity is the same. Consumers may be purchasing capacity, but the manufacturers are selling disks.

The capacity curve will pressure disk providers. Larger drives might not be in high demand for client machines as users opt for a smaller local disk and store additional data on a local network or in the cloud. This provides an opening for SSDs to hit a similar unit cost and prove attractive even for lower capacity. The speed, weight, ruggedness, and power requirements of a 512-gigabyte SSD may attract more customers than a four-terabyte disk. Having hit a "sweet spot" of $50 OEM (original equipment manufacturer) cost for a 128-gigabyte unit, solid-state will own most of the portable/laptop market and intrude into desktop workstations.

The enterprise market for magnetic disk drives comprises two categories of disk: high-performance drives (10K and 15K RPM) and high-capacity drives (four terabytes and larger). In contrast to the consumer market drives mentioned above, the enterprise category appears to be slightly more stable, but this group is facing challenges as well. High-performance disk drives are losing ground to SSDs. Specifically, high-performance drives tend to be closer in capacity to SSDs, making the pricing differential less significant. This downside, combined with the SSD's increased performance and smaller footprint, is drawing the attention of the enterprise storage community. In fact, at the time of this writing, shipments of high-performance drives were experiencing consistent quarterly decreases.

The future looks more promising for enterprise high-capacity drives. A comfortable price differential between these drives and

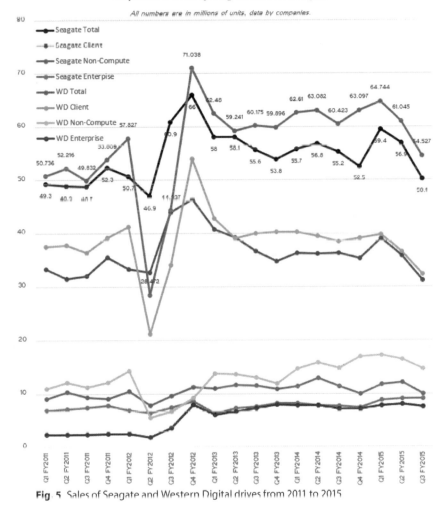

Fig. 5 Sales of Seagate and Western Digital drives from 2011 to 2015

SSDs is projected for several years, which will be important for the capacity enterprise disk market, such as cloud storage, which is one of the few safe havens we see for magnetic disk at this time. Market share in both high-performance and high-capacity enterprise drives will also be more sensitive to meeting the industry's projected roadmaps for capacity and performance gains.

Gaming and DVR devices are moving onto the cloud and therefore into the archive drive space. But as they and client drives do so, many smaller and sparsely populated drives will potentially be coalesced onto fewer larger drives managed by cloud providers.

The archive drive market is poised both to grow and to remain a stronghold of magnetic disk. Cloud providers will continue to require large numbers of high-capacity disks for immediate access and staging. Figure 5 shows published unit sales from Seagate and Western Digital from fiscal years 2011 through 2015, broken down into use category. Although capacity increased, unit shipments were flatter than anticipated and declined for several quarters.

Magnetic disk manufacturers have the steepest climb to achieve their roadmap capacities. SMR and helium-filled disk drives represent singular advances, unlike the iterative and repeatable improvements that have characterized the technology to date. Significant technical challenges are required to meet the published capacity estimates. Heat-assisted magnetic recording (HAMR) will be required to meet the areal densities projected through 2018. This technology has been positioned as being "right around the corner" by manufacturers as far back as 2007, so there is debate in the industry on its viability. Heated-dot magnetic recording (HDMR) and perhaps bit-patterned media (BPM) are expected to meet projections through 2025 and beyond if they can be brought to market. These technologies are working successfully under lab conditions, but their commercialization faces enormous risk. The largest and most vital storage medium—disk—faces the largest growth risk, which speaks to the importance of diversifying and planning for tiered storage layers.

Magnetic Tape

Magnetic tape traces its pedigree to the earliest commercialization of data processing. Everyone has seen stock footage of 1970s data centers with racks of nine-track reels spinning sporadically. Formats have since changed and  areal densities have increased exponentially, but tape retains economic and logistic advantages for archival storage and boasts good shelf life. As magnetic disk encroaches on tape's turf, however, many have questioned the future of tape storage. Looking at roadmaps for different technologies, an under-appreciated advantage of tape is its access to plentiful surface area. (Areal densities matter less when you have a mile of tape in a cartridge.)

In the case of disk and solid-state storage, technological breakthroughs are required to meet projections. Currently for both there appear to be limits not only of manufacturing but actual quantum considerations as bit densities approach small numbers of electrons.

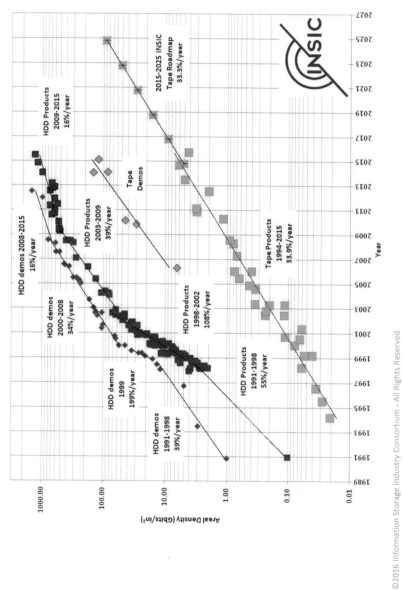

Fig. 6 Areal density trends from 1991 to 2015. (Chart provided courtesy of the Information Storage Industry Consortium [INSIC].)

IBM and Fujifilm have already demonstrated, in laboratory conditions, the areal densities that are required to meet the bulk of their published roadmaps. As Figure 6 shows, the 85.9-gigabyte-per-square-inch density could fulfill the roadmap through 2025. Aaron Ogus, Microsoft's partner development manager, has said that tape manufacturers are "sandbagging—they don't have to try to hit these densities."[6] This might be an exaggeration, but of all the types documented here, tape clearly requires less breakthrough technology. A six-platter 3.5-inch form-factor disk drive has approximately 99 square inches of recordable surface area. A half-inch magnetic tape cartridge has approximately 19,500 square inches of recording area, or nearly 200 times the recordable surface area of the disk drive.

Nevertheless, tape progress might find itself threatened more by demand than by supply. Spectra Logic's research has shown that midrange and small enterprise customers have been slower to adopt higher-density tape drives than have larger-sized organizations. Large cloud providers will continue to drive the market for future releases. The demand for higher capacity will come from fewer—albeit high-volume—customers. The midrange market will upgrade more slowly.

Large customers will demand higher capacity and although every manufacturer likes to please its largest customers, the demand lag could have an impact on product roadmaps. Certain high-capacity formats might further split off from the midrange and enterprise sectors if customers continue to be complacent with a shallower growth curve.

Solid-State Disk

Demand for SSD is bright, as seen in its expansion in application and its current status as the only storage medium seeing consistent revenue growth. In the portable computing segment, SSD is displacing magnetic disk and 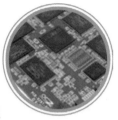 has no immediate rival in the categories of smartphones and tablets. It is expected that SSD will also be increasingly used in ultra-high-performance database applications and as a caching tier in network-attached RAID systems.

In the new set of storage tiers, SSD supplies a latency of sub-10 milliseconds for high-performance access. Magnetic disk is slower in comparison, but it still provides a respectable latency of sub-100 milliseconds. Large SSD drives are showing up in HADOOP clusters for highly transactional data and analytics performance, while magnetic disk is used for supporting information that is read-only or rarely changed.

As mentioned, SSD does not need to completely close its price differential with magnetic disk to continue intruding into the latter's segments. For most applications on notebook computers, unit costs matter more than does capacity; a smaller SSD disk is attractive for portability, performance, and power consumption. Additional storage—likely on magnetic disk, perhaps backed up on tape or optical media—is generally available on the cloud, a home storage area network (SAN), or on an enterprise network.

The limits of SSD will be felt more acutely in supply. Manufacturers face significant technical and manufacturing challenges in their continued efforts to increase capacity and lower costs. Although a significant spread in cost-per-capacity will limit some of the use cases in which magnetic disk is directly threatened, such as cloud storage, SSD continues to gain market share. An economical break-even point between SSD and magnetic disk does not appear to be on any manufacturer roadmaps.

Optical Disk

Optical storage adds greatly to storage diversity. As with tape media, optical media can be stored offline to protect it from power surges and equipment hazards, such as fire.  Optical and tape media can also be conveniently shipped far away to provide geographic diversity, and both offer media diversity from magnetic disk.

Optical storage also has a much longer shelf life and is less susceptible to environmental hazards. The biggest threat to optical storage is physical damage to the medium or substrate itself, whereas magnetic media can be harmed by induction. Despite its benefits, optical storage has supply and roadmap challenges: Densities need to be substantively increased and media costs reduced to further blur the lines with tape. Some vendors are looking at packaging optical media into cartridges that can be handled by automated libraries in the same way as is done with tape. Optical could then prove the more attractive choice for larger-capacity automated environments with denser packaging and storage options.

As the consumer market increasingly favors streaming over optical media for movies and music, there is some speculation that dormant production lines could be used to produce lower-cost optical storage media. Many of the suggested technologies could conceivably be produced on current manufacturing lines. The question here then is one of intent: Is it a good business model to produce low-margin, high-volume media?

To displace a large part of the tape market, optical would need to achieve media costs below $1 per terabyte by 2030, from about $30 per terabyte in 2015, an unrealistic expectation. The optical roadmap describes an increase to one terabyte per platter (from 300 gigabytes) by 2021, but nothing beyond that if using the existing, inexpensive substrate layer.

The Cloud as Media Type

For many consumers, cloud storage is an abstract concept that does not conjure up a physical media type. And while cloud storage is clearly not a media type apart from disk, tape, optical, or SSD, it functions as one. From the standpoint of diversity, cloud storage quickly and easily provides certain benefits, including offsite storage and potential geographic separation from a data center. Cloud storage customers include major organizations that are investing heavily in data protection and best practices, as well as smaller data centers that wish to efficiently outsource their IT concerns to a cloud provider.

However, cloud storage might not be right for every organization, since many of them might have protection and security concerns about having their data located offsite and out of their control. The cloud is an incredible resource but, as always, the topic of restoration brings up more difficult questions than does the problem of storage. In the event of major data loss, for example, how long would it take to recover data, how much would it cost, and what would the plan be for data that is unrecoverable?

Adding cloud storage as one element of diversity can be a good move, but one must consider the storage provider's practices, as well as service-level agreements and restoration costs. Keeping a copy of its data accessible allows an organization to maintain control when recovery is necessary, and it also prevents a single point of failure that would otherwise be under a vendor's control.

❧ ❧ ❧

No prediction suggests that the rate of data creation will abate. Rather, the discussion is more about orders of magnitude— will it be a lot or a whole lot of data? This distinction raises an additional risk regarding the sourcing and pricing of storage media and the allocation of a media portfolio across different technologies. Diversity in storage media allows allocations to be managed among different media as costs change.

Spectra Logic plans to periodically update the data storage projections provided in this appendix. Interested parties are invited to view and comment on these updates at www.spectralogic.com.

Notes

Chapter 1

1. Greg Easterbook, "Forgotten Benefactor of Humanity," *The Atlantic*, January 1997, http://www.theatlantic.com/past/issues/97jan/borlaug/borlaug.htm.

2. Jacob Bunge, "Big Data Comes to the Farm, Sowing Mistrust," *Wall Street Journal*, February 25, 2014, http://www.wsj.com/articles/SB1000142405270 23044509045793692838869192124.

3. *Wikipedia*, s.v., *Geography* (Ptolemy), accessed January 15, 2015, https:// en.wikipedia.org/wiki/Geography_(Ptolemy).

4. Frank J. Schwetz, "Mathematical Treasure: Bakhshali Manuscript," Mathematical Association of America, October 2015, http://www.maa.org /press/periodicals/convergence/mathematical-treasure-bakhshali-manuscript.

5. Frank Viviano, "China's Great Armada: Admiral Zheng He," *National Geographic*, July 2005, http://ngm.nationalgeographic.com/print/features/world/asia /china/zheng-he-text.

6. Ann Gibbons, "The Great Famine: Decoded," *Science Magazine*, May 21, 2013, http://news.sciencemag.org/biology/2013/05/great-famine-decoded/.

7. John Gantz and David Riensel, "The Digital Universe in 2020: Big Data, Bigger Digital Shadows, and Biggest Growth in the Far East," IDC iView (International Data Corporation), December 2012, http://www.emc.com /collateral/analyst-reports/idc-the-digital-universe-in-2020.pdf.

8. Robert Bready, "Downtime and Data Loss: How Much Can You Afford?" Aberdeen Group, 2013, http://www.aberdeen.com/research/8623 /ai-downtime-disaster-recovery/content.aspx.

9. John Gantz and David Reinsel, "The Digital Universe in 2020."

Chapter 2

1. "After 3D, Here Comes 4K," *The Economist: Technology Quarterly*, March 9, 2013, http://www.economist.com/news/technology-quarterly /21572921-home-entertainment-new-television-standard-called-ultra-hd -four-times-sharper.

2. Gantz and Riensel, "The Digital Universe in 2020" (see chap. 1, n. 7).

3. "Sharon Gaudin, "The Digital Universe Created 161 Exabytes of Data Last Year," *Information Week,* March 7, 2007, http://www.informationweek.com/the-digital-universe-created-161-exabytes-of-data-last-year/d/d-id/1052683.

4. Brian Dolan, "AT&T Develops 'Smart Slippers' for Fall Prevention," *MobiHealthNews,* December 7, 2009, http://mobihealthnews.com/5675/att-develops-smart-slippers-for-fall-prevention.

5. Andrew Atkeson and Patrick J. Kehoe, "The Transition to a New Economy After the Second Industrial Revolution" [Working Paper No. 8676], National Bureau of Economic Research, Cambridge, MA, December 2001, http://www.nber.org/papers/w8676.

6. Michael DeGusta, "Are Smart Phones Spreading Faster Than Any Technology in Human History?" *MIT Technology Review,* May 9, 2012, https://www.technologyreview.es/printer_friendly_article.aspx?id=40321.

7. Philip N. Howard, Aiden Duffy, Deen Freelon, Muzammil M. Hussain, Will Mari, and Marwa Maziad. "Opening Closed Regimes: What Was the Role of Social Media During the Arab Spring?" [PITPI Working Paper 2011.1], Project on Information Technology & Political Islam, University of Washington, Seattle, WA, 2011, p. 2, http://dx.doi.org/10.2139/ssrn.2595096.

8. Ibid, 4.

9. Gayle Osterberg, "Update on the Twitter Archive at the Library of Congress," Library of Congress [blog], January 4, 2013, https://blogs.loc.gov/loc/2013/01/update-on-the-twitter-archive-at-the-library-of-congress/.

10. Matt Raymond, "How Tweet It Is! Library Acquires Entire Twitter Archive," Library of Congress [blog], April 14, 2010, http://blogs.loc.gov/loc/2010/04/how-tweet-it-is-library-acquires-entire-twitter-archive/.

11. Leslie Johnston, "A 'Library of Congress' Worth of Data: It's All in How You Define It," Library of Congress [blog], April 25, 2012, http://blogs.loc.gov/digitalpreservation/2012/04/a-library-of-congress-worth-of-data-its-all-in-how-you-define-it/.

12. Ibid.

13. Osterberg, "Update on the Twitter Archive."

14. James Manyika, Michael Chui, Brad Brown, Jacques Bughin, Richard Dobbs, Charles Roxburgh, and Angela Hung Byers, *Big Data: The Next Frontier for Innovation, Competition, and Productivity,* (New York: McKinsey Global Institute, 2011), http://www.mckinsey.com/business-functions/business-technology/our-insights/big-data-the-next-frontier-for-innovation.

Chapter 3

1. Matt Ridley, *The Rational Optimist* (New York: Harper Collins, 2010), p. 56.

2. "Digestive Disorders Health Center: Picture of the Appendix," WebMD, http://www.webmd.com/digestive-disorders/picture-of-the-appendix.

3. Matt Ridley, *The Evolution of Everything: How New Ideas Emerge* (New York: HarperCollins, 2015), Kindle edition, location 1227-1230.

4. Viktor Meyer-Schönberger and Kenneth Cukier, *Big Data: A Revolution That Will Transform How We Live, Work and Think* (New York: Eaton Dolan, 2014).

5. *Wikipedia*, s.v., "Electronic Discovery," accessed January 20, 2015, https://en.wikipedia.org/wiki/Electronic_discovery.

6. Jay Livens, "Scary Statistics on SMB Data Backup," Iron Mountain, Inc., July 23, 2013, http://blogs.ironmountain.com/2013/service-lines/data-backup -and-recovery/scary-statistics-on-smb-data-backup/.

Chapter 4

1. Charles Roe, "The Growth of Unstructured Data: What to Do With All Those Zettabytes?" Dataversity, March 12, 2012, http://www.dataversity.net/the-growth -of-unstructured-data-what-are-we-going-to-do-with-all-those-zettabytes/.

2. Economist Intelligence Unit, "The Deciding Factor: Big Data and Decision Making," *The Economist*, London: Capgemini, 2012, p. 6.

3. Charles Duhigg, "How Companies Learn Your Secrets," *The New York Times Magazine*, February 16, 2012, http://www.nytimes.com/2012/02/19/magazine /shopping-habits.html.

4. "Gartner Reveals Top Predictions for IT Organizations and Users for 2014 and Beyond" [press release], Gartner, Inc., October 8, 2013, http://www.gartner .com/newsroom/id/2603215.

5. Tom McCall, "Understanding the Chief Data Officer Role," Gartner, Inc., February 18, 2015, http://www.gartner.com/smarterwithgartner/understanding -the-chief-data-officer-role/.

6. Zack O'Malley Greenburg, "The Rich Afterlife of Michael Jackson," *Forbes*, October 25, 2010, http://www.forbes.com/2010/10/21/michael-jackson-sony -business-entertainment-dead-celebs-10-jackson.html.

7. *Wikipedia*, s.v., "Supercomputer," accessed January 20, 2016, https://en.wikipedia.org/wiki/Supercomputer.

8. "The November 2015 List," TOP500, http://www.top500.org/2015/11/.

9. Alex Knapp, "How Much Does It Cost to Find a Higgs Boson?" *Forbes,* July 5, 2012, http://www.forbes.com/sites/alexknapp/2012/07/05/how-much -does-it-cost-to-find-a-higgs-boson/#1ff0ac3e64f0.

10. Cian O'Luanaigh, "CERN Data Centre Passes 100 Petabytes" [press release], European Organization for Nuclear Research, February 12, 2013, last modified March 12, 2015, http://home.cern/about/updates/2013/02/cern-data -centre-passes-100-petabytes.

11. Corinne Pralavorio, "LHC Season 2: CERN Computing Ready for Data Torrent" [press release], European Organization for Nuclear Research, June 2, 2015, http://home.cern/about/updates/2015/06lhc-season-2-cern -computing-ready-data-torrent.

12. Georgia Wells, "Facebook 'Likes' Mean a Computer Knows You Better Than Your Mother," *The Wall Street Journal,* September 11, 2015, http://blogs.wsj .com/digits/2015/09/11/facebook-likes-mean-your-computer-knows-you -better-than-your-mother/.

13. Faiza Sareah, "Interesting Statistics for the Top 10 Social Media Sites," *Small Business Trends,* July 26, 2015, http://smallbiztrends.com/2015/07/social-media -sites-statistics.html.

14. Ibid.

15. Dylan Tweney, "Facebook Explains Secrets of Building Hugely Scalable Sites," *Venture Beat,* September 16, 2013, http://venturebeat.com/2013/09/16 /facebook-explains-secrets-of-building-hugely-scalable-sites/12.

16. Brian McKenna, "What Does a Petabyte Look Like?" *Computer Weekly,* March 2013, http://www.computerweekly.com/feature/What-does-a-petabyte -look-like.

17. Sareah, "Interesting Statistics."

18. "Rising Volume of Medical Imaging Data to Increase the Adoption of Cloud Computing in the Healthcare Sector" [press release], MarketsandMarkets, http://www.marketsandmarkets.com/ResearchInsight/north-america -healthcare-cloud-computing.asp.

19. "U.S. Medical Imaging Informatics Industry Reconnects With Growth in the Enterprise Image Archiving Market" [press release], Frost & Sullivan, November 1, 2012, http://www.frost.com/prod/servlet/press-release .pag?docid=268728701.

20. "Personal Genomics: The Future of Healthcare?" Yourgenome, last modified June 19, 2015, http://www.yourgenome.org/stories/personal-genomics-the -future-of-healthcare.

21. Robert Gebelhoff, "Sequencing the Genome Creates So Much Data We Don't Know What to Do With It," *Washington Post,* July 7, 2015, https://www.washingtonpost.com/news/speaking-of-science/wp/2015/07/07/sequencing-the-genome-creates-so-much-data-we-dont-know-what-to-do-with-it/.

22. Zachary D. Stephens, et. al., "Big Data: Astronomical or Genomical?" *PLOS Biology,* vol.13, no. 7 (2015), doi: 10.1371/journal.pbio.1002195.

23. Francis S. Collins, Eric D. Green, Alan E. Guttmacher, and Mark S. Guyer, "A Vision for the Future of Genomic Research," *Nature,* vol.422, 835-847 (2003), accessed January 21, 2016, http://www.nature.com/nature/journal/v422/n6934/full/nature01626.html.

24. "Division of Genomics and Society," National Human Genome Research Institute, last updated July 1, 2015, http://www.genome.gov/27550080.

25. "Hubble's Top Breakthroughs" [multimedia presentation], HubbleSite, http://hubblesite.org/hubble_discoveries/breakthroughs/.

26. Peter Braam, e-mail to Nathan Thompson, March 20, 2016.

27. Rhys Newman and Jeff Tseng, "Cloud Computing and the Square Kilometre Array" [Memo no. 134], SKA Organization, May 2011, https://www.skatelescope.org/uploaded/8762_134_Memo_Newman.pdf.

28. Braam, e-mail.

29. Ibid.

30. "Project," Square Kilometre Array, https://www.skatelescope.org/project/.

Chapter 5

1. J. P. Blaho, "Want to Sell Disaster Recovery to Senior Management? Stop Saying 'Disaster,'" *Forbes,* October 28, 2013, http://www.forbes.com/sites/sungardas/2013/10/28/want-to-sell-disaster-recovery-to-senior-management-stop-saying-disaster/.

2. Linda Park, "Data Breach Trends," Symantec Connect, December 13, 2013, http://www.symantec.com/connect/blogs/data-breach-trends.

3. Raymond Boggs, Randy Perry, and Jean Bozman, "Reducing Downtime and Business Loss: Addressing Business Risk With Effective Technology," IDC, August 2009, http://www.hp.com/hpinfo/newsroom/press_kits/2009/CompetitiveEdge/ReducingDowntime.pdf.

4. Park, "Data Breach Trends."

5. "Worst Storm Damage Ever Rips Con Edison Equipment" [press release], Con Edison, October 30, 2012, http://www.coned.com/newsroom/news /pr20121030.asp.

6. John-Paul Kamath, "Disaster Planning and Business Continuity After 9/11," *Computer Weekly,* September 11, 2007, http://www.computerweekly.com /news/2240082860/Disaster-planning-and-business-continuity-after-9-11.

Chapter 6

1. "Malware Statistics," AV-TEST Institute, January 28, 2016, https://www .av-test.org/en/statistics/malware/.

2. SINTEF, "Big Data, for Better or Worse: 90% of World's Data Generated Over Last Two Years," *ScienceDaily,* http://www.sciencedaily.com/releases /2013/05/130522085217.htm.

3. Brian Krebs, "Adobe to Fix Another Hacking Team Zero-Day," *Krebs on Security,* July 16, 2015, http://krebsonsecurity.com/2015/07/adobe-to-fix -another-hacking-team-zero-day/.

4. Chester Wisniewski, "CryptoLocker, CryptoWall and Beyond: Mitigating the Rising Ransomware Threat," Sophos, 2015, https://universalframeworks .com/wp-content/uploads/2015/06/UFI-partner-sophos-cryptowall- cryptolocker-ransomware-wpna.pdf.

5. John Zorabedian, "Anatomy of a Ransomware Attack: CryptoLocker, CryptoWall, and How to Stay Safe" [infographic], Sophos [blog], March 3, 2015, https://blogs.sophos.com/2015/03/03/anatomy-of-a-ransomware-attack -cryptolocker-cryptowall-and-how-to-stay-safe-infographic/.

6. "Ransomware," Trend Micro, accessed January 26, 2016, http://www .trendmicro.com/vinfo/us/security/definition/ransomware.

7. "Meet 'Tox': Ransomware for the Rest of Us," McAfee Labs [blog], March 23, 2015, https://blogs.mcafee.com/mcafee-labs/meet-tox-ransomware-for -the-rest-of-us.

8. Wisniewski, "CryptoLocker, CryptoWall and Beyond."

9. Brian Krebs, *Spam Nation: The Inside Story of Organized Cybercrime—from Global Epidemic to Your Front Door,* (Chicago: Sourcebooks, 2014) p.173.

10. "The Top 10 Worst: The World's Worst Spammers," Spamhaus, April 16, 2016, https://www.spamhaus.org/statistics/spammers/.

11. Jonathan Weisman, "U.S. Shifts Stance on Drug Pricing in Pacific Trade Pact Talks, Document Reveals," *The New York Times,* June 10, 2015, http:// www.nytimes.com/2015/06/11/business/international/us-shifts-stance-on -drug-pricing-in-pacific-trade-pact-talks-document-reveals.html?_r=1.

12. David Kushner, "The Masked Avengers," *The New Yorker*, September 8, 2014, http://www.newyorker.com/magazine/2014/09/08/masked-avengers.

13. "Hector Monsegur Interview Part 3: Sony's Hack and Sabu's Next Steps," *CNET* video, 12:40, December 15, 2014, http://www.cnet.com/videos/hector-monsegur-interview-part-3-sonys-hack-and-sabus-next-steps/.

14. Kushner, "The Masked Avengers."

Chapter 7

1. "The Global Regime for Transnational Crime" [issue brief], Council on Foreign Relations, http://www.cfr.org/transnational-crime/global-regime-transnational-crime/p28656.

2. Annelise Anderson, *The Red Mafia: A Legacy of Communism*, (Stanford, CA: The Hoover Institution Press, 1995), http://www.auburn.edu/~mitrege/FLRU2520/RedMafia.html.

3. David C. Jordan, *Drug Politics: Dirty Money and Democracies* (Norman, OK: University of Oklahoma Press, 1999).

4. "Cyber's Most Wanted," Federal Bureau of Investigation, accessed January 10, 2016, https://www.fbi.gov/wanted/cyber.

5. Mansur Mirovalev and Colin Freeman, "Russian Hacker Wanted by U.S Hailed as Hero at Home," *The Telegraph*, June 7, 2014, http://www.telegraph.co.uk/news/worldnews/europe/russia/10883333/Russian-hacker-wanted-by-US-hailed-as-hero-at-home.html.

6. Ibid.

7. Michael Riley, "Neiman Marcus Breach Linked to Russians Who Eluded U.S.," *Bloomberg*, April 7, 2014, http://www.bloomberg.com/news/articles/2014-04-07neiman-marcus-breach-linked-to-russians-who-eluded-u-s-.

8. Mae Anderson, "Hacker Heist: Russian Hacking Ring Steals $1 Billion from Banks," *The Christian Science Monitor*, February 16, 2015, http://www.csmonitor.com/USA/Latest-News-Wires/2015/0216/Hacker-heist-Russian-hacking-ring-steals-1-billion-from-banks.

9. "Feds Say Five Hackers Stole 160 Million Credit Card Numbers in Largest Data Theft Case Ever Prosecuted in the U.S." *Daily Mail*, July 25, 2013, http://www.dailymail.co.uk/news/article-2378322/Feds-say-hackers-stole-160-Million-credit-card-numbers-largest-data-theft-case-prosecuted-U-S.html.

10. David Goldman, "The Cyber Mafia Has Already Hacked You," *CNNMoney*, July 27, 2011, http://money.cnn.com/2011/07/27/technology/organized_cybercrime/.

Notes

11. Isaac Porsche III, "Cyberwarfare Goes Wireless," *U.S. News & World Report,* April 4, 2014, http://www.usnews.com/opinion/blogs/world-report/2014/04 /04/russia-hacks-a-us-drone-in-crimea-as-cyberwarfare-has-gone-wireless.

12. Amy Thomson and Cornelius Rahn, "Russian Hackers Threaten Power Companies, Researchers Say," *Bloomberg,* July 1, 2015, http://www.bloomberg .com/news/articles/2014-06-30symantec-warns-energetic-bear-hackers-threaten -energy-firms.

13. Scott Pelley, "FBI Director on Threat of ISIS, Cybercrime," *CBS News,* October 5, 2014, http://www.cbsnews.com/news/fbi-director-james-comey -on-threat-of-isis-cybercrime/.

14. Andrea Shalal and Matt Spetalnick, "Data Hacked from U.S. Government Dates Back to 1985—Official," *Reuters,* June 5, 2015, http://www.reuters .com/article/2015/06/05/cybersecurity-usa-iduskbn0ok2IQ20150605.

15. Jeff Stein, "Exclusive: Chinese Cyberthieves Hack FBI in Dangerous Breach," *Newsweek,* June 24, 2015, http://www.newsweek.com/china-hackers-fbi -346667.

16. Ellen Nakashima, "Chinese Hack of Federal Personnel Files Included Security-Clearance Database," *The Washington Post,* June 12, 2015, http://www .washingtonpost.com/world/national-security/chinese-hack-of-government - network-compromises-security-clearance-files/2015/06/12/9f91f146-1135 -11e5-9726-49d6fa26a8c6_story.html.

17. Damian Paletta, "When Does a Hack Become an Act of War?" *The Wall Street Journal,* June 13, 2015, http://www.wsj.com/articles/when-does-a-hack -become-an-act-of-war-1434189601.

18. Sean Gallagher, "Why the 'Biggest Government Hack Ever' Got Past the Feds," *Ars Technica,* June 8, 2015, http://arstechnica.com/security/2015/06 /why-the-biggest-government-hack-ever-got-past-opm-dhs-and-nsa/.

19. Natasha Bertrand, "The Massive Chinese Hack of US Security Clearance Info Keeps Getting Worse," *Business Insider,* June 19, 2015, http://www .businessinsider.com/the-massive-chinese-hack-of-us-security-clearance-info -keeps-getting-worse-2015-6.

20. Franz-Stefan Gady, "New Snowden Documents Reveal Chinese Behind F-35 Hack," *The Diplomat,* January 27, 2015, http://thediplomat.com/2015/01 /new-snowden-documents-reveal-chinese-behind-f-35-hack/.

21. Jose Pagliery, "Ex-NSA Director: China Has Hacked 'Every Major Corporation' in U.S.," *CNNMoney,* March 16, 2015, http://money.cnn .com/2015/03/13/technology/security/chinese-hack-us/.

22. Ibid.

23. Ibid.

24. Dave Lee and Nick Kwek, "North Korean Hackers 'Could Kill,' Warns Key Defector," *BBC,* May 29, 2015, http://www.bbc.com/news/technology-32925495.

25. Christine Kim, "Defector Claims North Grooms Hackers," *Korea JoonAng Daily,* June 2, 2012, http://koreajoongangdaily.joins.com/news/article/article.aspx?aid=2937036.

26. David E. Sanger and Martin Fackler, "N.S.A Breached North Korean Networks Before Sony Attack, Officials Say," *The New York Times,* January 18, 2015, http://www.nytimes.com/2015/01/19/world/asia/nsa-tapped-into-north-korean-networks-before-sony-attack-officials-say.html?r=0.

27. Samuel Gibbs, "New Sony Pictures Hacking Demand Strengthens North Korea Link," *The Guardian,* December 9, 2014, http://www.theguardian.com/technology/2014/dec/09/new-sony-pictures-hacking-north-korea-link.

28. John Gaudiosi, "Why Sony Didn't Learn from Its 2011 Hack," *Fortune,* December 24, 2014, http://fortune.com/2014/12/24/why-sony-didnt-learn-from-its-2011-hack/.

29. Julianne Pepitone, "Massive Hack Blows Crater in Sony Brand," *CNNMoney,* http://money.cnn.com/2011/05/10/technology/sony_hack_fallout/.

30. Michael Cieply and Brooks Barnes, "Sony Cyberattack, First a Nuisance, Swiftly Grew Into a Firestorm," *The New York Times,* December 30, 2014, http://www.nytimes.com/2014/12/31/business/media/sony-attack-first-a-nuisance-swiftly-grew-into-a-firestorm-.html.

31. Matthew Garrahan, "Sony Cyber Attack Reveals Hackers Changing Their Stripes," *Financial Times,* December 5, 2014, https://next.ft.com/content/1c967b94-7c0d-11e4-a7b8-00144feabdc0.

32. Chris Strohm, "Sony Hack Signals Threat to Destroy Not Just Steal Data," *Bloomberg,* December 5, 2014, http://www.bloomberg.com/news/articles/2014-12-04/sony-hack-signals-emerging-threat-to-destroy-not-just-steal-data.

Chapter 8

1. Robert Johnson, "Boeing Now Has a Missile That Destroys Only Electronics and Leaves All Else Intact," *Business Insider,* October 25, 2012, http://www.businessinsider.com/beoings-counter-electronics-high-power-microwave-advanced-missile-project-2012-10.

2. *Wikipedia,* s.v., "Starfish Prime," accessed March 27, 2016, https://en.wikipedia.org/wiki/Starfish_Prime.

3. William Radasky and Edward Savage, "Intentional Electromagnetic Interference (IEMI) and Its Impact on the U.S. Power Grid," Metatech Corporation, January 2010, http://www.ferc.gov/industries/electric /indus-act/reliability/cybersecurity/ferc_meta-r-323.pdf.

4. "Electromagnetic Compatibility (EMC), Part 2-13: Environment—High-power Electromagnetic (HPEM) Environments—Radiated and Conducted," International Electrotechnical Commission, March 9, 2005, https://webstore.iec .ch/publication/4131.

5. Radasky and Savage, "Intentional Electromagnetic Interference."

6. Henry F. Cooper and Peter Vincent Pry, "The Threat to Melt the Electric Grid," *The Wall Street Journal,* August 30, 2015, http://www.wsj.com/articles /the-threat-to-melt-the-electric-grid-1430436815.

7. David B. Jackson, "Intentional Electromagnetic Interference: Leapfrogging Modern Data Center Physical and Cyber Defenses," *Mission Critical,* August 16, 2010, http://www.missioncriticalmagazine.com/articles/82416 -intentional-electromagnetic-interference-leapfrogging-modern-data-center -physical-and-cyber-defenses.

8. R. James Woolsey and Peter Vincent Pry, "The Growing Threat from an EMP Attack," *The Wall Street Journal,* August 12, 2014, http://www.wsj.com /articles/james-woolsey-and-peter-vincent-pry-the-growing-threat-from-an -emp-attack-1407885281.

9. Patrick Thibodeau, "New Data Center Protects Against Solar Storms and Nuclear EMPs," *Computerworld,* September 15, 2014, http://www.computerworld.com /article/2606378/new-data-center-protects-against-solar-storms-and-nuclear -emps.html.

10. Patrick Cockburn, "War With Isis: Islamic Militants Have Army of 200,000, Claims Senior Kurdish Leader," *The Independent,* November 15, 2014, http:// www.independent.co.uk/news/world/middle-east/war-with-isis-islamic -militants-have-army-of-200000-claims-kurdish-leader-9863418.html.

11. "Terror Threat Snapshot" [multimedia graphic], House Committee on Homeland Security, accessed January 25, 2016, https://homeland.house.gov/map/.

12. Hannah Kuchler, "Warning Over Isis Cyber Threat," *Financial Times,* September 18, 2014, https://next.ft.com/content/92fb509c-3ee7-11e4-adef-00144feabdc0.

13. Ibid.

14. "Inside TAO: Documents Reveal Top NSA Hacking Unit," *Der Spiegel,* December 19, 2013, http://www.spiegel.de/international/world/the-nsa-uses -powerful-toolbox-in-effort-to-spy-on-global-networks-a-940969.html.

15. Andrea Peterson, "Are Squirrels a Bigger Threat to the Power Grid Than Hackers?" *Washington Post,* January 12, 2016, https://www.washingtonpost.com/news/the-switch/ wp/2016/01/12/are-squirrels-a-bigger-threat-to-the-power-grid-than-hackers/.

16. Pavel Polityuk, "Ukraine Sees Russian Hand in Cyber Attacks on Power Grid," *Reuters,* February 12, 2016, http://www.reuters.com/article/us-ukraine-cybersecurity-iduskcn0vll8e.

17. Steve Reilly, "Bracing for a Big Power Grid Attack: 'One Is Too Many,'" *USA Today,* March 24, 2015, http://www.usatoday.com/story/news/2015/03/24/power-grid-physical-and-cyberattacks-concern-security-experts/24892471.

Chapter 9

1. Nicholas Nassim Taleb, *Black Swan: The Impact of the Highly Improbable* (New York: Random House, 2007); *Antifragile: Things That Gain from Disorder* (New York: Random House, 2012).

2. Todd Hoff, "How Google Backs Up the Internet Along With Exabytes of Other Data," High Scalability, February 3, 2014, http://highscalability.com/blog/2014/2/3/how-google-backs-up-the-internet-along-with-exabytes-of-othe.html.

3. Andrew Tanenbaum, *Computer Networks,* 4th ed., (London: Pearson, 1981), p. 91.

4. Randall Monroe, "FedEx Bandwidth," What If? http://what-if.xkcd.com/31/

Chapter 10

1. Sydney Brenner, "Refuge of Spandrels," *Current Biology,* vol. no. 8 (1998), http://www.sciencedirect.com/science/article/pii/S0960982298704270.

2. Robert Guthrie, "Interesting Facts About the CGI Used in Avatar," Avatar Blog, May 24, 2010, http://avatarblog.typepad.com/avatar-blog/2010/05/learn-about-the-different-special-effects-used-in-the-making-of-avatar-the-movie.html.

3. Kathy Benjamin, "Mindhole Blowers: 20 Facts About Gone With the Wind That Will Make You Give a Damn," Pajiba, May 16, 2012, http://www.pajiba.com/think_pieces/mindhole-blowers-20-facts-about-gone-with-the-wind-that-will-make-you-give-a-damn.php.

4. Yelena Aronova-Tiuntseva and Clyde Freeman Herreid, "Hemophilia: 'The Royal Disease,'" National Center for Case Study Teaching in Science, University at Buffalo, State University of New York, (1999), last updated 2003, http://sciencecases.lib.buffalo.edu/cs/files/hemo.pdf.

Appendix

1. Ridley, "The Evolution of Everything," (see chap. 3, n. 3), Kindle location 816-822.

2. Mick Jason, "If Intel and Micron's 'Xpoint' Is 3D Phase Change Memory, Boy Did They Patent It," *Daily Tech,* July 29, 2015, http://www.dailytech.com/exclusive+if+intel+and+microns+xpoint+is+3d+phase+change+memory+boy+did+they+patent+it/article37451.htm.

3. Dexter Johnson, "The Memristor's Fundamental Secrets Revealed," *IEEE Spectrum,* June 6, 2013, http://spectrum.ieee.org/nanoclast/semiconductors/nanotechnology/the-memristors-fundamental-secrets-revealed.

4. George M. Church, Yuan Gao, and Sriram Kosuri, "Next-Generation Digital Information Storage in DNA," *Science,* doi: 10.1126/science.1226355, http://phys.org/news/2012-08-dna-encode-digital.html.

5. *Wikipedia,* s.v., "An Essay on the Principle of Population," accessed April 13, 2016, https://en.wikipedia.org/wiki/An_Essay_on_the_Principle_of_Population.

6. Stephen Lawson, "IBM, Fujifilm Cram 220TB of Data Onto Tape-based Storage That Fits in Your Hand," *PC World,* April 10, 2015, http://www.pcworld.com/article/2908652/ibm-fujifilm-show-tape-storage-still-has-a-long-future.html.

Bibliography

Many similarities exist between genetic diversity in natural evolution and in data. If you wish to dig deeper into this topic, the excellent works of science and technology that are quoted in this book are worth investigating.

Genetics and Evolution

Bray, Dennis. *Wetware: A Computer in Every Living Cell*. New Haven: Yale University Press, 2011.

Collins, Francis S. *The Language of God: A Scientist Presents Evidence for Belief*. New York: Simon & Schuster, Inc., 1997.

Dawkins, Richard. *The Selfish Gene*. Oxford: Oxford University Press, 1976.

Dawkins, Richard. *River Out of Eden: A Darwinian View of Life*. London: Weidenfeld & Nicolson, 1995.

Ridley, Matt. *Genome: The Autobiography of a Species in 23 Chapters*. New York: HarperCollins, 2013.

Cosmology

Deutsch, David. *The Beginning of Infinity: Explanations That Transform the World*. New York: Penguin Books, 2001.

Deutsch, David. *The Fabric of Reality*. New York: Viking Adult, 1997.

Ridley, Matt. *The Rational Optimist*. New York: HarperCollins, 2011.

Wilczek, Frank. *A Beautiful Question: Finding Nature's Deep Design*. New York: Penguin Books, 2015.

Yau, Shing-Tung, and Steve Nadar. *The Shape of Inner Space: String Theory and the Geometry of the Universe's Hidden Dimensions*. New York: Perseus Books Group, 2011.

Bibliography

Technology and Human Society

Hidalgo, Cesar. *Why Information Grows: The Evolution of Order, from Atoms to Economies.* New York: Basic Books, 2015.

Krebs, Brian. *Spam Nation: The Inside Story of Organized Cybercrime—from Global Epidemic to Your Front Door.* Chicago: Sourcebooks, Inc., 2014.

Lazear, Edward P. *Economic Transition in Eastern Europe and Russia: Realities of Reform.* Stanford, CA: The Hoover Institution Press, 1995.

Mayer-Schönberger, Viktor, and Kenneth Cukier. *Big Data: A Revolution That Will Transform How We Live, Work and Think.* Boston: Houghton Mifflin Harcourt, 2013.

Munroe, Randall. *What If? Serious Scientific Answers to Absurd Hypothetical Questions.* Boston: Houghton Mifflin Harcourt, 2014.

Pinker, Steven. *The Better Angels of Our Nature: Why Violence Has Declined.* New York: Penguin Books, 2011.

Ridley, Matt. *The Evolution of Everything: How New Ideas Emerge.* New York: HarperCollins, 2015.

Taleb, Nassim Nicholas. *Antifragile: Things That Gain from Disorder.* New York: Random House, Inc., 2012.

Taleb, Nassim Nicholas. *Black Swan: The Impact of the Highly Improbable.* New York: Random House, Inc., 2007.

Illustration Credits

Chapter 1

Image on page 1: Adobe Stock.

Figure 1: "Ptolemy World Map," from Ptolemy's the *Geography*, redrawn by Francesco di Antonio del Chierco (15th century). Housed in the British Library, London. Image retrieved from https://commons.wikimedia.org/wiki /File:PtolemyWorldMap.jpg.

Figure 2: Diagram of hard-disk drive manufacturer consolidation. Image © Juventas, CC-BY-SA 3.0. Retrieved from https://commons.wikimedia.org /w/index.php?curid=16149377.

Chapter 2

Images on pages 15 and 18: Adobe Stock.

Figure 1: "Exponential Growth of Computing for 110 Years." Image from Ray Kurzweil's, "The Future of Moore's Law," Kurzweil: Accelerating Intelligence. Retrieved from http://www.kurzweilai.net/ask-ray-the-future-of-moores-law.

Figure 2: "Social Networking in the Arab World." From *Media Use in the Middle East*, 2013, © 2013 Northwestern University in Qatar. Retrieved from http:// menamediasurvey.northwestern.edu/#.

Chapter 3

Image on page 29: Adobe Stock.

Figure 1: IBM logo evolution. Image retrieved from http://www.retireat21.com /entrepreneurship/17-evolutions-of-logos#IBM_Logo_Evolution.

Chapter 4

Images on pages 41, 46, and 50: Adobe Stock.

Figure 1: Large Hadron Collider. Image © CERN. Retrieved from http://home .cern/topics/large-hadron-collider.

Figure 2: Bibliotheca Alexandrina. Image retrieved from https://en.wikipedia.org /wiki/Bibliotheca_Alexandrina, available under CC0 1.0, (universal public domain).

Illustration Credits

Image on page 60: Adobe Stock.

Figure 3: "Cost per Genome" chart based on data presented by Kris Wetterstrand, "DNA Sequencing Costs: Data from the NHGRI Genome Sequencing Program," National Human Genome Research Institute. Retrieved from http://www.genome .gov/sequencingcosts/.

Figure 4: Artist's rendition of SKA-mid dishes in Africa. Image © 2015 SKA Organization. Retrieved from https://www.skatelescope.org/wp-content /uploads/2011/03/SKA1_SA_closeup_midres.jpg.

Figure 5: Artist's rendition of low-frequency antennas in Australia. Image © 2015 SKA Organization. Retrieved from https://www.skatelescope.org/multimedia /image/ska-low-frequency-aperture-array-close-up-australia/.

Chapter 5

Image on page 69: Adobe Stock.

Figure 1: USB drive. Image: Adobe Stock.

Figure 2: South Ferry subway station, Lower Manhattan. Image: MTA New York City Transit/Leonard Wiggins.

Chapter 6

Image on page 79: Adobe Stock.

Figure 1: "Total Malware in Existence" chart adapted from "Total Malware" chart © AV-TEST GmbH. Retrieved from https://www.av-test.org/en/statistics /malware/.

Figure 2: Web snapshot of Tox graphical interface. Image from "Meet 'Tox': Ransomware for the Rest of Us," McAfee Labs. Retrieved from https://blogs .mcafee.com/mcafee-labs/meet-tox-ransomware-for-the-rest-of-us/snapshot.

Figure 3: Botnet diagram. Image retrieved from http://cybersuriya.blogspot .com/2013/09/hello-guys-in-this-tutorial-ill.html.

Figure 4: "Anonymous logo (Perfect Symmetry)." Image © 2013–16 by anondesign. Retrieved from http://anondesign.deviantart.com/art/Anonymous-Logo-Perfect -Symmetry-408648867.

Chapter 7

Image on page 95: © Spectra Logic Corporation.

Figure 1: FBI most-wanted poster (Bogachev). Image: Federal Bureau of Investigation. Retrieved from https://www.fbi.gov/wanted/cyber/evgeniy-mikhailovich-bogachev.

Figure 2: FBI most-wanted poster (Chinese military officers). Image: Federal Bureau of Investigation. Retrieved from https://www.fbi.gov/news/news_blog/five-chinese-military-hackers-charged-with-cyber-espionage-against-u.s.

Chapter 8

Image on page 111: Adobe Stock.

Figure 1: CHAMP. Image © Boeing. Retrieved from http://www.businessinsider.com/beoings-counter-electronics-high-power-microwave-advanced-missile-project-2012-10?0=defense.

Figure 2: USS *Forrestal*. Image: United States Navy (Catalog no. USN 1124794). Retrieved from http://www.history.navy.mil/our-collections/photography/numerical-list-of-images/nara-series/usn/USN-1120000/USN-1124794.html.

Figure 3: Low-power EMP gun kit. Retrieved from http://www.amazing1.com/emp.html.

Chapter 9

Images on page 129: Adobe Stock.

Figure 1: Amazon Web Services™ S3 logo © Amazon Web Services, Inc. All rights reserved.

Figure 2: Storage media types. Image: Adobe Stock

Figure 3: "Earthquakes Since 1898, by Magnitude" designed by John Nelson. Image © www.IDVsolutions.com. All rights reserved. Retrieved from http://uxblog.idvsolutions.com/2012/06/earthquakes-since-1898.html.

Chapter 10

Image on page 141: Adobe Stock.

Figure 1: *Gone With the Wind* poster. Image © Warner Bros. Entertainment Inc. All rights reserved.

Figure 2:. "Checksumming Ulysses" © Spectra Logic Corporation.

Appendix

Figure 1: "Digital Universe: Storage Worldwide" graph, taken from *Digital Data Storage Outlook 2016*, © 2016 Spectra Logic Corporation.

Figure 2: Photograph © Rusty Vision. Combined graphic © 2016 Spectra Logic Corporation.

Figure 3: "Media Tiers" chart © Spectra Logic Corporation. Images: Adobe Stock.

Figure 4: "LTO Roadmap" based on publicly available data from the LTO Consortium. Image © Spectra Logic Corporation.

Image on page 171: Adobe Stock.

Figure 5: "Shipments of HDDs by Seagate and Western Digital" graph. Image retrieved from http://www.kitguru.net/components/hard-drives/anton-shilov /shipments-of-hard-disk-drives-hit-multi-year-low-in-q1-2015/.

Image on page 175: Adobe Stock.

Figure 6: "Areal Density Trends" graph © Information Storage Industry Consortium. All rights reserved.

Images on pages 178 and 179: Adobe Stock.

About the Authors

Nathan C. Thompson is the CEO of Spectra Logic Corporation, which has its roots in Western Automation, a manufacturer of memory boards, peripheral test equipment, and storage systems that Nathan founded in 1979 and ran while earning his B.S. degree in electrical engineering and computer science from the University of Colorado Boulder.

In 1988, Western Automation acquired the assets of the interface company Spectra Logic and, in 1996, the combined company was renamed Spectra Logic Corporation. Today, Spectra Logic is a leading manufacturer of innovative tape and disk-based data backup and archive solutions, with products installed globally in more than 40 countries.

Active in local business and civic communities, Nathan is a member, since 1984, and chairman of the Rocky Mountain chapter of the Young Presidents' Organization, as well as a member of both the World Presidents' Organization and the Colorado Thirty Group. Nathan also serves on the University of Colorado's Electrical Engineering Advisory Board and on the Finance and Investment Committee of the Alexander Dawson School in Lafayette, Colorado.

In 1996, Ernst & Young and *USA Today* named Nathan "Entrepreneur of the Year," and in 2003 he was awarded the Distinguished Engineering Alumni Award (DEAA) from the University of Colorado. He was inducted into the Boulder County Business Hall of Fame in April 2012.

Nathan enjoys collecting and restoring vintage pinball machines and is also a licensed commercial instrument pilot with more than 2,300 flight hours logged.

Bob Cone has more than 30 years of experience in the data storage industry, including in sales, product management, and corporate training, which he brings to his role as technology evangelist at Spectra Logic Corporation. Bob's primary focus is on the many industry challenges related to long-term data storage. He applies his knowledge and practical expertise to developing critical insights into these problems, as well as to investigating other areas of impact, such as matters of compliance, new data-reduction technologies, digital preservation for "non-IT–related" data storage, and the "store forever" concept.

A frequent speaker, Bob is widely recognized for his keen observations on industry trends, which he shares with his audiences so that they might apply new technologies and methods to addressing their current data storage and preservation challenges, as well as meeting future storage needs.

John Kranz is a software developer at Spectra Logic Corporation and a 30-year veteran of the data storage industry. He has an avid interest in cosmology, popular science, and economics. Regarding his participation in *Society's Genome,* John has stated, "This project spoke not only to my work, but also to my appreciation for modernity and human advancement."